FROM
HIP HOP TO HOLLYWOOD:
THE ART OF CHRISTIANITY

A NEW MILLENNIUM PERSPECTIVE ON CHRISTIANITY AND THE ARTS

FROM HIP HOP TO HOLLYWOOD: THE ART OF CHRISTIANITY

BY

BRADY GOODWIN JR.

From Hip Hop to Hollywood: The Art of Christianity

Copyright © 2013 Brady Goodwin, Jr.

Self-Published by Brady Goodwin through Urbanremixproject.com

Philadelphia, PA

Cover Art by Shareece Alexander
Cover Design by Judeus Samson

Edited by Donna Wyche

Printed in the United States of America by Createspace

ISBN-10: 0988415518
ISBN-13: 978-0-9884155-1-5

TABLE OF CONTENTS

DEDICATED TO:

THE CREATIVITY OF THE CREATOR'S CREATIVE CREATURES WHO CREATE THEIR OWN CREATIONS AND CONFOUND US WITH THEIR FEATURES

MAKE YOURSELF AT HOME

"Hip Hop was my home I had my shoes off"

In his song "Chase That," the rap artist Lecrae used these words to describe his early years as a resident of Hip Hop culture. But, by the time he recorded this phrase in 2010, Lecrae had become the new face of a twenty year old counter-culture known as Christian Hip Hop or, alternatively, Holy Hip Hop.

This counter-culture housed individuals who, like Lecrae, once felt totally at home in Hip Hop culture but, had also come to genuine faith in Jesus Christ. These redeemed Hip Hoppers soon found that they felt just as at home, if not more so, in Christ. Many wondered, however, what it would be like for someone who now had his abode in Christ to venture back across that seemingly real, though possibly imagined line between secular and sacred rap to, once again, make himself at home in the secular Hip Hop arena.

For years, the common hope among leaders in the Christian Hip Hop community had been to witness the day when the broader culture would open its doors to Christian rappers. But, rarely, were any outspoken Christians allowed to rest inside of Hip Hop's pimped-out-palace. And, if ever they did gain re-entry, they were certainly not allowed to kick off their shoes and put their feet up on the culture's cushiony couch. For, it was obvious that these "Christian rappers" were no longer at home and were now without honor in their hometown.

But what if someone could actually do it? What if someone whose foot-fashion was laced with the 'preparation of the Gospel of peace' were to be welcomed back into "Run's House?" Would this individual be forced to take those Gospel-gripping shoes off at the door as he entered or would he be able to still proudly proclaim Christ?

After all of the strides made to represent Jesus and stick a flag in the ground for the Christian faith and the God of the Bible, would the one who dared to cross back over the line have to jettison his Christian title and/or function in order to be welcomed in that world? And if so, would the Christian community still support such an artist or would we be torn amongst ourselves concerning the legitimacy of the mission?

These were all hypothetical questions until 2012—the year when several, formerly-known-as, Christian rap artists began making intentional moves to insure that they would end up in front of the very crowds that most Christian rappers were writing to but, quite honestly, never physically ending up in front of.

Before this time, Lecrae, along with countless other Christian rappers, would have instantly credited the pioneering group, *The Cross Movement*, for directly or indirectly mentoring his efforts in urban musical ministry. The Cross Movement, of which I was a member for fourteen years, championed the 'no-shame' approach to representing Jesus in Hip Hop. We stood as full fledge Hip Hoppers and indigenous missionaries, not as outsiders who had "become all things to all men."

We made authentic, top-notch, East-coast Hip Hop music. And, at the same time, we stood for authentic, Christ-centered, Bible-based Christianity. There was no shame of the person of Jesus but, also, there was a certain pride in being young, urban Christians who were active in Hip Hop yet, still strongly connected to the people of God.

This strong stance had affected many changes:

- Many who, at first, could not imagine how the Christian faith was supposed to work in the inner-city became convinced that it could and converted to the faith
- Closet-Christians out of the closet as the shame of being a Christian in the urban context was eliminated
- The charges of urban cult-religions against Christians and Christianity were forcefully and convincingly answered
- An industry that, previously had no room for Christian Hip Hop began to make room

There was B.E.T. airplay, *Source* magazine articles and Grammy nominations among others, but none of that was sought and all of that was peripheral to the mission of calling those whom God had called and blessing those God would bless. However, in 2007, The Cross Movement officially signed off and handed the baton to the next generation of Christian MCs.

At first, these new rappers embraced the formula of those who had gone before them. It was this pro-Christ/pro-Christian formula, excellence in artistry, shrewdness in business, along with the new "Roman Roads" of social media that helped them reach heights of which The Cross Movement had only dreamed.

But it soon became obvious that the old formula was no longer preferred by some. Interview after interview and explanation after explanation began to reveal the belief that simply excellence in artistry and business, along with the Roman Roads of social media, mixed with the right relationships in the industry would be the keys to success going forward. Or, at least, that's what the public was being told. Yet, some of these artists were saying one thing, and doing another.

Their explanations argued for a certain freedom and liberty in art. And yet, their continued success, at least among their Christian fan base, still seemed to be hinged on the communication of Christian beliefs. The freedom for which they argued would come in the form of a few innovative moves, such as the doing away with the Christian title and certain partnerships which might have been unthinkable while operating under that title. But what else might these formerly-known-as Christian artists be gearing up for?

Their interviews left many confused and concerned. Should the success of Christian art and artists going forward be based on these new ideas?

Were these ideas really that new? Where were these artists getting these ideas from? And, would these ideas work the same with an urban art-form such as Hip Hop as they might for other cultural art-forms that play by different rules?

Many young artists were eager to try to employ the strategy being voiced by these formerly-known-as Christian artists. As one of the pioneers of the Christian Hip Hop movement, my social network inboxes began flooding with questions from those who have followed these artists for years but were now getting confused by their methods. I offered a balanced perspective as, to the surprise of many, I often co-signed the questionable missionary efforts of these young, urban musical ministers. Despite this, I agreed with those asking the questions, that there was a cause for concern and a need for caution.

I have now chosen to address these issues and more, not because I am in total disagreement with all of the moves being made by my peers and successors; but because the explanations being given by some of these artists do not seem safe if left unaddressed. The reasons being offered might or might not lead to the missteps of those who are offering them. But they will certainly impact others who are looking to build their artistic careers on the new foundations being laid by today's Christian leaders in the world of modern art.

I am thinking not only of those artists who are currently believers and struggling with these game-changing decisions; but, also of anyone who may come closer to Christ as a result of these new moves being made by today's Christian artists. On the one hand, if anyone comes closer to Christ—Amen! But suppose a person has only come nearer to Christ because he or she has seen our artists shed their connection to Christ or Christ's community (Christians = the Church) for the sake of success. Will this produce a different breed of disciple than Christianity and even Christian Hip Hop has seen in the past?

We know that, as Christians, our "sold-out-ness" to Christ, Christ's cause and Christ's community has kept many unbelievers at bay. But, those who have been drawn to the Savior by our strong statements and strong stances have come this way with the understanding of the high price of discipleship. They came and switched up careers, tore up contracts, broke up connections, burned up cd collections, and gave up conditions and any other thing that would hinder them from full fledge devotion to Jesus Christ. I have witnessed this for twenty years and, to this day, still hear these types of testimonies from many.

My desire is that these testimonies do not become a thing of the past, especially for the sake of, or in the name of "art."

However, I realize that it is not just Christian rappers who struggle with the issues which will be addressed in this book. Christians who are actors, dancers, songwriters, play wrights, script writers and filmmakers alike, have all expressed dismay when reconciling their faith to their passion for the arts in the twenty-first century.

So, while this book was spawned by issues specific to Christianity and the art of Hip Hop music, i.e., rap; it has expanded to cover a variety of issues and principles that should be helpful for anyone dealing in any of today's modern art forms. I admit that these principles are not as firm as law but, they are just a bit stronger than opinion. They point to a biblical and God glorifying path forward through a very confusing subject. Keep an open mind and an open heart. Be prepared also to open your Bible. Then, kick off your shoes and make yourself at home.

Introduction

1. A NAME FOR OURSELVES

Is it right or wrong for Christian artists to "water down" their message for the sake of reaching more people? Is it acceptable for someone to remove the title "Christian" from what he/she does in order to reach more people? Can a Christian just do good art and not have to be concerned with reaching the lost artistically?

These are not just "gotcha" questions thrown out to draw you, the reader, into a controversial book. These are real questions being asked by sincere, modern artists who care deeply about the answers. The answers will impact decisions waiting to be made right now or first thing tomorrow morning as artists, nationwide, prepare to write their next check to an agent, sign a contract with a manager, step into the studio, onto a stage or sit in front of a camera to record their next promo video.

Part of me wishes I could simply respond with a straight 'yes' or 'no' but that would not satisfy any serious inquiry. And yet, any thoughtful reply will only open up more issues and lead to other questions which will demand more thoughtful answers. It has been my pleasure to think through these important issues and organize the arguments and responses in a way that, I pray, will be most helpful to those who are asking these and similar questions.

My answers revolve around my understanding of two key topics: culture and art. Art is a product of the soul but it is produced for the benefit of a culture. Each culture then has the privilege of presenting its artistic gifts to the world. But, as the world shrinks and technology gives us ever-increasing ways to share artifacts from one culture to the next, artist can now bypass their culture and present their art directly to the world.

Still, those from within an artists' own culture; those who helped to inform and shape the artistic values of that culture and those who live by those values, will gravitate to the artist's production the most and even inform the broader world audience on how to best receive and evaluate the art.

Take, for instance, improvisational jazz. No one comes to this art-form from the outside and attempts to critique it. Instead, we sit first and learn the ways of jazz; understand the cultural art; then, and only then, does one begin to understand how to evaluate it. So it is with the issues addressed in this book. It will be important to keep in mind that, it is not just the cultures of various modern art-forms that must be understood; but Christianity is, itself, a culture that must be understood if we are to properly address the challenges and opportunities facing today's Christian artists.

Therefore, we cannot simply begin with art. In order to see our way clear, we need to do a very difficult thing. We need to talk about the role and importance of 'culture' in an individualistic age where everyone is free to do what's right in his/her own eyes. Until then, talking about art will do us no good. In America, where pop-culture has replaced mom & pop culture and values are dispensed by the media instead of the immediate family, all sorts of ideas about art have come to us across the airwaves.

When we take our cue from these sources, we tend to judge the success of works of art by how popular or profitable they are instead of the productivity and spiritual fruit they yield. Whenever a culture's art is judged this way it has already become commercialized and will soon cease to benefit the culture it was intended to serve. The art might still have the ability to entertain us, but it will more than likely only amuse. And there is a major difference between the two.

To 'entertain' means to hold ones attention; to cause someone to think, focus or fixate on a certain point. But the word 'amuse' is interesting. It means to divert ones attention; to cause someone to look away or not to think about a certain thing. We will soon see that the purpose of art is to cause us to think about a very specific thing. It is because of this purpose that art and amusement are actually antithetical. They oppose one another. Therefore, any culture whose art simply amuses has lost a great deal.

Now, I'm sure that, whatever a culture may lose when its art-forms are commercialized might seem like a small price to pay. The loss will especially seem inconsequential if the artists behind the art get to rise from poverty and obscurity in the process. However, when we see the strong link between culture and art, we will begin to understand how high a price is really paid when the one is detached from the other. So, before we dive into the subject of art, let's start by getting both a biblical and sociological understanding of culture.

Culture in the Bible

The most basic definition of culture is "A shared way of life." The definition gets a bit lengthy when you begin to enumerate the things individuals who are in the same culture share with one another. But from the first book of the Bible, Genesis, we see an important aspect of shared life-ways (culture). Genesis 1:28 is commonly referred to as "the cultural mandate." Here, God commands the man and woman that he created to: 1. Be fruitful and multiply; 2. Fill the earth up with other people and other things based on the raw materials given by God; and 3. Subdue the earth and have dominion over it, or, make it serve their purposes.

We learn some additional information about culture later on in Genesis. By the time we reach chapter 11, even though there were many more people on the face of the earth, it appears that there were not yet many people groups; many cultures. In fact, it could be argued that there were not yet *ways* of life, but only a shared way of life—one culture.

Genesis 11:1 tells us that the whole world spoke one and the same language. And even though people were beginning to move and migrate toward the west, when they began to build the tower of Babel and make a name for themselves God saw that the whole earth, not just a segregated people group was getting ready to succeed in an unauthorized mission. He therefore confused man's language and men were forced to spread out from there, huddling up into the various groups of people which began to produce the cultural diversity we see today.

This suggests that culture, and not cultures, was the original state. But then, in the New Testament, we find something even more interesting. The idea of countless cultures around the world was not an afterthought in the mind of God. In the book of Acts, we learn that the multiplication of cultures was actually designed by God in order to create a problem that would lead man back to God as the solution.

In fact, in Genesis 11, when mankind shared one common language and, presumably, one common culture, men perceived a problem. They were worried about being scattered and nameless. Instead of subduing the earth, they feared that the earth might subdue them. Their solution was a tower; a monument in their own name. But, God had a problem with their solution and so, he gave them a new problem—a bigger problem, i.e. cultures. The different languages forced men to huddle up with those whom they could understand and develop ways of life that were distinct from other groups of people with different languages.

In Acts 17, however, we learn that the reason God

determined and designated the different places and times that men should live was because God desired to use the elements of each person's time and setting (culture) as a means to cause us to look outside of where we have been placed in order to, perhaps, find God, though he is not far from each one of us (Acts 17:27). Apparently, there is something about the ways of life being offered to us by the world's variety of cultures that causes us to "grope" for God.

And God knew where and when to place each one of us. He knew which culture, be it Hip Hop or Hippie, would best serve his purpose for you and me. In Matthew 28, Jesus gives the Great Commission telling his disciples to go into all the world's manifold cultures knowing that each and every culture has prepared each and every person to seek for something more than what their culture has to offer. When we understand this, we will do a better job of reaching out to other cultures and we may even become more effective witnesses for Christ within our own.

A Sociological View of Culture

On top of this biblical understanding, we can add a sociological view of culture. This will help us to identify the specific ways in which each individual culture ultimately leaves each individual person searching for more (groping for God). Uncovering this information becomes much less difficult when we know the "cultural questions."

In my first book, *The Death of Hip Hop, Marriage & Morals*, I give the following definition and explanation of culture under the subheading *What's* and *Ways*:

Culture [refers to] the *ways* different groups of people come together to answer life's *what's*; or life's questions. From culture to culture, the *ways* may change, but the *what's* hardly ever do. Here is a list of the *what's* that lead to our different *ways*.

- **Food** (What to eat and how to prepare it?)
- **Fashion** (What do we do to cover the body and protect it from adverse elements and unauthorized eyes?)
- **Language/Lingo** (What can we do to make communication easier for those inside our group while keeping outsiders at bay?)
- **Art** (What events, emotions or ideas are worth reproducing and how expertly or uniquely can this be done?)
- **Values** (What do we do to preserve, perpetuate and progress our way of life? e.g., technology, dating, mating, law and order)
- **Ultimate Questions** (What is our Origin? Destiny? Meaning?)
- **Heroes** (Who among us, living or dead, has helped to answer these questions most?

- **Historic Events** (What are the memorable moments when these questions were answered for us? And how do we celebrate or commemorate those moments? e.g. holidays)

The heroes of a culture are the ones who are most well-known for answering these questions. The historic events are the timeless moments when these questions were answered. Often times, a culture's heroes are artists who answer these questions through their art. Some artists are famous for answering the *what* part of the art question (what's worth reproducing); others are simply famous for answering the *how* or the *ways* portion of the question (how expertly or uniquely can something be reproduced).

The Christian artist should not settle for only answering the *ways* aspect; but, rather, should be known for introducing the culture to new answers to the *what* aspect of the question of art. More on this in the next chapter.

Look again at the cultural questions above. The questions, and their answers, are all inter-related. But which ones are the most important? Those would be the 'values questions' and the 'ultimate questions'. These two tie the rest of them together. In fact, the more a group of people can tie the other questions and answers into these two, the stronger their culture will be. The more unrelated the answers to these questions are, the weaker their culture will be.

In the case of Hip Hop, it is easy to see how, once these answers became detached from the values questions, the culture's art was quickly and easily commercialized, commoditized and capitalized on. It has become, mostly, amusement. When listening to mainstream Hip Hop music, we are not made to think about or focus on what really matters. Our attention is diverted as the art often gives us awful answers to the question, 'what's worth reproducing?'

Culture and the Missionary

The failure to understand the links between these cultural questions and answers will lead to all sorts of missteps when attempting to reach a specific culture with the Gospel message. For this reason, I, along with the team of urban musical ministers with whom I was raised in ministry, The Cross Movement, have always believed in approaching the arts, even Hip Hop art, as missionaries and not simply as musicians. Doing this immediately cut out some of the confusion concerning 'just what is it okay to do in the name of reaching more people?'

If the Christian artist is not, at the same time, a missionary via the arts, then the questions at the beginning of this chapter do not even apply. But, for artists who are determined to be missional (be about the Great Commission), things can get a little tricky when dealing with different cultures. To be fair though, it is not just Christians in the arts who have struggled to be good missionaries. In times past, even bona fide, full-fledge, full-time Christian missionaries have failed to be good missionaries.

Historically, as Christian missionaries traveled to foreign lands and encountered new cultures, they struggled to rightly distinguish between the *what's* and *ways* of the people groups they sought to reach. Too often, they were unwilling or unable to recognize that it was only the answers to certain *what's* or certain *ways* about a particular culture with which they had a (biblically) legitimate issue. As a result, they attacked almost every foreign idea they encountered and eventually ended up discrediting or destroying all the *ways* of the peoples they were trying to reach.

This approach has led to many embarrassing moments in Christian missions and, even more recently, might explain why inner-city churches have had such a hard time reaching the Hip Hop culture right outside of its door. In his book *Let the Nations be Glad*, pastor/author John Piper has cautioned against the tendency for Christians to plant our own flowerpot (the *ways* we carry the Gospel) in other cultures instead of simply planting the flower of the Gospel (the *what* that's truly worth reproducing).

Though things have gotten tremendously better concerning foreign missions, there is still a lot of ground to be made up when it comes to homeland missions in America; especially as it relates to inner-city, youth culture or pop-culture. The pendulum often swings from one extreme to the other. The temptation is to either reject everything the culture has to offer, or else, accept it all with no questions asked. Both extremes lack a proper grid for determining whether or not certain facets of the culture are actually redeemable.

Caught in the Middle

Often, and mainly within the older generation, the church is caught in the middle of this pendulum swing and ends up in an awkward pose. This occurs when the church throws out things from, let's say, 'pop-culture' that are actually redeemable, e.g. tattoos, certain styles of dress, banning the wearing of ball caps in the church; but, also, at the same time, accepts things from the culture that are not redeemable, e.g. certain terminology, such as pastors or youth pastors shouting "YOLO" (You Only Live Once) to the crowd on Youth Sunday in an attempt to connect with younger members of the congregation.

But, this kind of cultural confusion is understandable when considering the generational gap between elders in the church and the youth culture of today. What is less conceivable is the way that certain formerly-known-as Christian artists today seem to be vying for an unnecessary re-categorizing of things which are redeemable and other things which are not.

Whether or not these artists believe what they are actually saying, they mislead others when they argue, "I'm a Christian; my music is not. My art does not have a faith; I do." This, they say, in their attempts to justify removing the Christian title from their art. But these artists have overlooked a very basic biblical principle. Not just people, but things can be redeemed as well. In Acts chapter 10, God told Peter not to call anything unclean that God himself has cleansed. The ultimate point of the passage did concern people (Gentiles who were seen as unclean by Jews) but the principle was just as true for the previously unkosher animals-for-food that God used as an example.

The term "cleansed" in that passage carried a ceremonial sense, taken from Israel's history of worshiping God in the Temple. Within that temple, all sorts of vessels and utensils were consecrated and made holy (set apart) to be used by the priest. God sanctifies things for his use. And once he sanctifies them, they are no longer common or to be used in a common way. Beyond this, Romans chapter 8 tells us that not just people and things but, all of creation is waiting and groaning for the redemption, of which the sons of God are the key manifestation.

The earth that was meant to be subdued under the Cultural Mandate of Genesis 1:28, and everything that sprang from it, is to be redeemed and brought back into one culture, a holy culture that sanctifies all of the various sub-cultures which can be found within it. This is the outcome of the Great Commission according to the book of Revelation chapter 7, verses 9 and 10. There, we learn that in the presence of the Lamb at the culmination of all things, believers will still be distinguishable by people groups and cultural differences. This means that our earthly cultures can and will be part of the redemption. And if art is a property of culture, then it follows that our cultural art forms can and will be redeemed as well.

The church is slowly coming to realize that this principle even applies to Hip Hop culture and art. But, how sad would it be if, just as the church is beginning to accept this fact; Christian artists, particularly those from the Hip Hopper culture who are the ideal missionaries to that culture, are beginning to lose sight of this biblical principle, all in the name of "art" or, in the name of "reaching more people?"

The Artist, the Mandate and the Mission

The Cultural Mandate of Genesis 1 produced an earth filled with people groups striving to answer the cultural questions. As different cultures come into contact with one another, they share their answers to these questions; be it art or fashion or values. Today we are able to share our answers with one another at an exponential rate through the new 'Roman Road' of social media.

But the result of the Great Commission is an earth being overrun with Christians who now have better answers to some of the key cultural questions (values and ultimate meaning). And, our answers to these key questions should influence our responses to the other cultural questions; specifically, that of art, as we look to share our answers with those in our own culture and with the rest of the world.

Does this make the Christian's art any better than the non-Christian's? Maybe, or maybe not. We will address this issue in the final chapter. But, at the very least, even if the Christian's answer to the *how* aspect of the art question is not any better, his answers to the *what* aspect (what is worth reproducing) should be.

Jesus told his disciples to go everywhere, teaching men everything that he had taught them. The Cultural Mandate had no real sense of urgency. The Great Commission does. The Mandate had limitless potential but was limited and sandbagged by man's sin, as seen in the Tower of Babel. But, for the Commission, we are given unlimited power which is if the gift of the indwelling Holy Spirit. The Spirit of God would not be needed if the Cultural Mandate were the only mission we were called to. Un-believers, without the Spirit of God, fulfill the Cultural Mandate every day.

Therefore, the artist, who is also a Christian, has missed the point of the Gospel if he lives as if he is only called to fulfill the Cultural Mandate. He has, in fact, traded in the New Testament of the Bible for a new tower of Babel. He might make a name for Himself, like the men of Genesis 11 were trying to do; but just like them, he may also find his communication becoming increasingly confusing to those around him.

As artist, we must wrestle with the fact that God is out to make a name for *his* self and to have us identify with that name. One of the aspects of the Great Commission is baptism in Jesus' name. Though many of us will never baptize another human being, one of the key concepts behind baptism is being identified with Jesus, according to Romans chapter 6. All of us can call others to be identified with Jesus and, thereby, come closer to fulfilling this facet of the Great Commission.

If this is the case, Christians who are artists have an amazing opportunity, an advantage even, if they leverage their platform to bring others not simply to the knowledge of Jesus, but to become identified with him; to name his name and, forsaking all others (the world at large), to join the throng that is his bride, i.e. the church. I use this marriage terminology on purpose for it is to this, we are called and to this we call others.

Now, there are a number of ways for a Christian to go about this "call." And as artists, the possible *ways* are so numerous that we should not expect two different artists to make the call in the same exact way. But, having explored the concept of culture, we can turn our attention to the subject of art in detail as we begin to work our way through some of the key questions burning on the hearts of modern artists. While we do this, as an artist or, simply as a Christian, you must answer for yourself whether you are simply functioning under the Cultural Mandate or under the Great Commission.

2. ONE MAN'S TREASURE: DEFINING AND DEFENDING ART

What is 'art' or 'artistic'? Does all art have to have a message or can I just do art for art's sake? Is there a difference between a Christian's art and Christian art?

In the last chapter I suggested that Jesus' commission to his disciples, "Go into all the world," makes the Christian a missionary wherever he or she goes. This is because, no matter where the Christian ends up, the Christian has not just gone, but has been sent. But now we must ask, 'do the arts qualify as a place that we have been sent into?' Some may argue for the ability to put the Great Commission on hold while they pursue their craft. Others will argue against that position. However, I believe that we will get further in this dialog once we have defined art and, if we can defend our definition.

This is definitely a touchy subject. When we speak about art, the temptation is to reduce it to an individualistic issue. In this way, each person can create or consume whatever he/she deems artistic and no one can challenge that person's call. How then can we instruct Christians as a whole, concerning how they ought to deal with this private subject? Is it even possible to assign a purpose to art that will serve as a guiding rule for Christians everywhere? I believe it is but, only if we do not detach art from its cultural significance.

Art and Values

Think about the cultural question of art introduced in the previous chapter: What events, emotions or ideas are worth reproducing and how expertly or uniquely can this be done? Consider how many cultures, especially on the continent of Africa, have traditionally linked the question of art to the cultural question of 'values' and 'ultimate meaning.'

This can be seen or, rather heard, clearly in the songs of some of these cultures. The drums are an artist's reproduction of the hearts beating. In song, there is often the idea that something ancestral is happening vocally. The sounds or tones are, in some way, reproducing, recalling or re-emoting the lives of those who have gone before. The music that comes from this way of life has given us what we know of today as soulful music.

Unfortunately, this is where many missionaries have committed the misstep of the 'all or nothing' approach—either accepting it all or rejecting it all. But this does not usually happen in the area of cultural food. And it is not often done in the area of language/lingo. Missionaries readily trade these artifacts with other cultures, believing that they are doing good missionary work as they learn the ways of those they desire to reach with the Gospel.

However, when it comes to how the missionary deals with fashion and art, there is still much room for improvement. The reason that so many have stumbled in this area is because of the close connections between a culture's fashion and art; and more importantly, because of the connections between a culture's art and its values.

It is because art aims to answer the question "What's worth reproducing," that art at its best is connected to the question of values. But if the missionary is not a fan of a culture's answers to the 'values' questions, then he/she will likely have a hard time with that culture's art and, possibly, the fashion of that culture as well.

Any culture that has weak answers to the 'values' questions; or, that has disconnected its art from its answers to the 'values' questions, will eventually lose its ability to come up with beneficial answers to the *what* aspect of the 'art' question (was it worth reproducing). As a result, that culture will end up only producing esthetically pleasing amusement instead of artful entertainment.

Therefore, the aim of the missionary should be to either: help a culture to develop better answers to the 'values' and 'ultimate' questions; or, to help a people group reconnect the cultural question of art to those two key cultural questions.

What is Artistic?

Art can be judged in one of two senses. It is both a *what* and a *way*. When Christian missionaries fail to properly appraise art it is usually because they fail to acknowledge the second sense. When Christian artists fail to produce quality art, it is usually because they pay too little attention to this same factor. Both the missionary and the Christian artist, however, usually pay close attention to the first sense. Interestingly, many nonbelievers pay great attention to the second sense and very little to the first.

But despite our individualistic society, I maintain that art is a cultural question which challenges us, as a society, to address the first and the second sense as we answer the questions, 'what's worth reproducing *and* how uniquely or expertly can that subject be reproduced.' Whenever an artist attempts to respond to these questions, his/her society will evaluate the artist's answers.

This can become tricky if the artist is taking his/her art directly to the world-stage, where many people may not understand the artist's culture. Nonetheless, during the evaluation process, there will be no shortage of people who differ in their opinion on the *ways* aspect of the artist's answers. But how about the *what* aspect; should we expect wide-reaching consensus regarding this sense of the artist's answers?

If beauty is in the eye of the beholder and one man's trash is another man's treasure, can we really expect there to ever be universal agreement on *what* is worth reproducing? Or, do those slogans about the subjective nature of beauty and treasure only apply to the *ways* aspect of art? Are we all just as free to esteem value and ascribe praise, not simply to the *how*, but to *what*ever strikes our own soul as fully artistic in both senses? If an individual likes horses or flowers or thunderstorms, won't that person think that a painting on one of these subjects is more worthy of reproduction than someone else who does not treasure his favorite things?

Perhaps; but there is a reason that we all ask the same questions when giving ourselves to, or, accepting what an artist is trying to give us through, a work of art. We usually ask two existential questions—as to being; and two esthetic questions—as to beauty. The four questions are 1.) What is this art an imitation of? (what does this remind me of or make me think/feel?) 2.) Is the subject of this art something worth reproducing or imitating and why or why not? 3.) How did the artist reproduce this concept; i.e. what technique(s) did the artist use? 4.) How well did the artist reproduce the concept?

The subject could be something very concrete, such as a sunset over a lake. The subject could also be an intangible quality, such as, the sense of wonder or bewilderment; an emotional state captured by certain musical notes or by the pace of the notes being played. In some works, the subject is more abstract, like the concept of symmetry, parallelism or contrast. And sometimes, as with Abstract Expressionist art, we struggle to put a finger on just what it is the artist was trying to reproduce. In these cases, the art becomes to us a reproduction of whatever we wish, since we are often at a loss as to what the piece originally meant to the artist who created it. We will return to this idea in just a moment.

But, no matter how gifted a painter or musician may be, there are some things that we struggle to call 'art.' I am not referring to those cases where we cannot tell what the work is a reproduction of. I am, rather, referring to those pieces which reproduce things that ought not to be mimicked. Even with the finest brush-strokes, it is counter-artistic to paint a portrait of something that is not worth reproducing, such as rape or a child being inappropriately touched.

Even in scenes or songs of rage or woe, we automatically read some justifiable quality into the work in order to deem it artistic (worth reproducing). So, when we interpret a violent painting of a stabbing, we choose to see it as a crime of passion, perhaps, motivated by love or, maybe revenge and, therefore, perhaps, the theme is justice—but not simply cold-blooded murder.

When we watch T.V. shows like *Dexter* [a serial killer who preys on other serial killers] or movies like the *Saw* series, we justify watching such brutality because the killer "has his reasons." Murder is not worth reproducing; love or justice, however, is. Even rage has its place in art, if the rage being reproduced is because of something truly outrageous and not simply because an individual chooses not to control his/her emotions.

Instinctively, we look for reasons in works of 'art' in order to be able to deem them 'artistic.' In this sense, the beauty *is* in the eye of the beholder because we refuse to let ourselves behold something *as* beautiful that really *is not* worthy of reproduction. In our desire to behold beauty, there is even, what I call, 'inverted art.' With inverted art, the piece tells us or challenges us to figure out what's worth reproducing, not by showing it to us, but by causing us to ask, "What's missing?"

A painting of a dilapidated project housing building might make us think of charity or social responsibility. Not because it is seen within the piece, but because it is missing. The same piece might stir up hope; the hope that something good might still come from such a place. Or, perhaps, pity or maybe shame that, as a society, we could have such scenarios playing out in our own backyards. Hope not hopelessness; pity though not simply the pitiful, or shame about the present circumstance that propels us into action in the future: all of these are worth reproducing. Even, if it is done in an inverted manner.

But, consider the point stated above; once the cultural question of art is disconnected from the cultural questions of values and ultimate meaning, the answers to the 'art' question can begin to make much less sense. 'What's worth reproducing' can be anything at all if we are not, at the same time, trying to preserve and perpetuate our way of life and if we do not know our purpose and destiny. This is why Hip Hop's musical art-form, rap, has gone to where it now lies, content-wise. Some people take issue with the style of popular rap (old school versus new; lyrical versus punch-line rap, underground versus commercial) but, the real issue at hand is not the *ways*, rather, it is the *whats*.

The church, along with "purists" from Hip Hop generation I (born between the mid-sixties and mid-eighties) miss their opportunity to address the waywardness of modern-day Hip Hop music by not distinguishing between their problem with the *ways* and their problems with the *whats* of Hip Hop generation II.

The Highest Art from the Highest Artist

Now that we have a working definition of culture and art, we can turn our attention to another pertinent question: is all art intentional? Does it always come from an artist communicating a message about what is worth reproducing? Consider the old saying: "All art is propaganda." Is this always the case?

Perhaps you are tempted to respond, "No." For, one can find beauty and the semblance of worthy subjects even in something as random as the ripples in a puddle or the shape of a cloud. But even then, don't we often wonder if it is merely a coincidence or, if, perhaps, the cloud has been formed by some divine sculptor for our viewing pleasure?

But why do we do this? It is because we are, by nature, interpreters of art. We are interested in knowing just what was worth reproducing in the eyes of the artist, even when no human hands can be found as the source of the work. But why are we so concerned about the subject, subtext and source of art? Why is it such a part of the human soul? Well, consider the fact that mankind is, before anything else, high art. In fact, it could be argued that we are the highest art from the hand of the highest artist because mankind is God's way of answering the question of art.

God is the chief artist because, in making man, God has reproduced the most worthy subject matter that could ever be reproduced. In Genesis 1:26, the Triune God said, "Let us make man in our likeness and in our image." The fact that God imaged himself in mankind means that humanity is an artistic creation and an expression. Man is the most artistic creation because there is no greater answer to the question, 'what's worth reproducing' than God himself. And so, it is precisely because we are artistic creations that we are also artistic creators.

Our inborn desire to create is matched by our inborn desire to interpret. God has designed it so that, if we rightly interpret ourselves, (the divine artwork we are) we will be forced to focus on the one whose image we were made to reflect. Each of us should ask ourselves, 'If I am a work of art, what's so artistic about me? What subject was so worth reproducing that I now exist?' And we should be thrilled to be able to answer back, "God! God is my subject matter."

But, because of our sinfulness, we fail to do this. We still manage to see ourselves and other human beings as wonderful works of art. But we interpret ourselves as 'art for art sake'. Not for God's sake. We love the *way* that we are. But we do not acknowledge the *what* which lies behind our design. This failure to rightly interpret mankind handicaps our ability to produce and interpret all other art; including that which we find within the various cultures we encounter and endeavor to reach.

But thankfully, there is one higher than us. Jesus is not an artistic creation for he always existed. Still, he is the expressed image, or exact imprint of the nature of God the Father (Hebrews 1:3). He is not a reproduction, for there was never a time when the Father was not expressing himself in the person of the Son (John 1:1,2). But, in the Father's eyes, he is worthy of reproduction. It is because we are flawed image bearers and have become poor answers to the question 'what's worth reproducing,' that God in his grace has determined to remake us after the image of the Son (Colossians 3:10), thereby reproducing Jesus in us.

How, then, should we answer the question, 'Is art always intentionally designed to communicate something about what's worth reproducing?' I believe that the answer is 'yes.' Whether or not the artist realizes that this is what he is doing is not the issue. The issue at hand is the nature of art. The instant anyone determines to do something artistic, he has taken up a moral challenge to find a worthy subject to reproduce. This challenge stems not from the artist's intention alone, but from the fact that we, as his audience have been created to instinctively interpret his art; not to be amused by it, but to ask the artistic questions and, perhaps, arrive at God or godliness as the chief subject and answer.

An Old Woman or a Beautiful Young Lady

Earlier in this chapter, I mentioned a certain kind of art called "Abstract Expressionism" where one cannot easily tell what the artist is attempting to reproduce. There is so much art in the world today that seems to be either super subliminal or so abstract, to the point that we as the viewing/listening public get to make of it whatever we want. Because this kind of art is "in vogue," we must ask the question, 'Can the Christian who is using the arts to communicate his faith, afford to produce this type of unintentional, abstract expression?' But we must also distinguish between the subliminal and that which is purely abstract expressionistic.

Have you ever seen the portrait of the old, haggard woman and the young beauty? It is not two images but one. The same lines form both images at the same time. There is nothing about the work of art which has to change in order for you to see something different within the frame. The only thing that has to change is your perspective. It is quite the optical illusion.

When you first stare at this piece, you may not even be aware of what you are looking at. But soon, some part of it will catch your eye and inform you that there is a woman to behold. The artist has intentionally conveyed the two images in hopes that you will eventually realize that there is more than just the one. If you never perceive the second image on your own, perhaps someone else will come along and help you to see it. But, even if not, at least it is there, waiting for you to discover it. This is the subliminal approach to art. I believe that many more Christians who are artists need to learn this skill.

However, with Abstract Expressionism, meaning is not simply difficult to immediately decipher; it is utterly "up for grabs." The artwork may have been the reproduction of some definite thing in the eyes of the artist, but that artist is perfectly okay if it means something completely different to you. In fact, the work is so non-distinct that, unless the artist is right there with you to interpret it or has left his explanation, you would never know for certain what it meant to him in the first place.

For the Christian who is also an artist to produce this kind of art and expect someone to arrive at a God-centered destination, the artist must make a major overestimation, either of his own ability to preach the Gospel without really preaching it or, of the human heart's ability to arrive at divine truth without clear communication. Yes, God can take our unclear communication and still communicate his truth through it, but that is his intentionality at work in spite of us. This should not serve as a license for artists to be unclear or unintentional.

Art History

But why does this unintentional (let the viewers or listeners decide what the message means to them) style of art appeal to us so much today? This is normally not an issue when dealing with the art-form of rap music. Rap can be subliminal and abstract, but not quite abstract expressionistic. It is much more likely to be overly overt.

It seems that it is more common for the artistic meaning to be left up to the public when it comes to the visual art of painting and sometimes film. But, for reasons that will be discussed in the next chapter, more and more Christians, be they rappers or film makers, are tempted to borrow this stylistic approach, not from the Bible or Christian history, but from the descendants of the Enlightenment period.

The 15th through the 17 century, in Western Europe, marked a period of return to classical Greek and Roman ideas, art and architecture. This period also welcomed a challenge to *tradition and religion* in the secular world (The Renaissance), and a challenge to *traditional religion* in the Church (The Reformation).

Before this time, the church controlled everything and every facet of life, including government and the arts. But the Renaissance and Reformation allowed the various institutions of society to break free from the church and develop lives of their own. This was not an altogether bad thing. For in many cases, it was not the church controlling government, but government controlling society through the church.

The cultural component of the arts really enjoyed the newfound freedom of the Renaissance. Instead of painting strictly religious-themed works, like the Sistine Chapel or sculpting works like the statue of David, artists could now expand their subject matter into the wide, wild world of Greek mythology. This was a welcomed change of pace from the monotony of the biblically significant.

However, not long after breaking free from the creative tyranny of the Catholic Church, artists soon realized that they were not yet free enough. For in dealing with Greek mythology, artists had gone from only reproducing the works of God to now only reproducing the works of the gods. But, through the Renaissance, man's focus had shifted from an emphasis on God to an emphasis on man as "the measure" or "measurer of all things." But how could artists capture this theme and reflect that their society's answers to the ultimate cultural questions had changed from God to man?

One answer came toward the end of the 19th century in the form of impressionist art. Here, the focus was not to capture and convey the subject matter itself but, rather, to convey the experience of the human eye in the process of seeing. Instead of being concerned with the works of God, artists, and painters in particular, were now concerned with the experience of man.

Following this came post-impressionist art which began to distort images and use unnatural colors chosen at the painter's whim. This gave artists a taste of autonomy. But the real answer came several decades later in the form of Abstract Expressionism. The name is a spinoff from German Expressionism which arose in the early 20th century while Germany was isolated from the rest of the world during World War I. That nation produced a slew of dark movies that dealt with the psychosis and madness that can accompany life at times, especially during *that* time.

Abstract Expressionism, which has its origins in America, is that style of art which causes us to stand and tilt our heads from side to side as we try to imagine just what it is that we are staring at. The most we are able to take away from the world is some grasp on the concept of color coordination or repetition of a certain pattern or, possibly, the use of a certain painting technique. But, unless the artist tells us that the piece is called "Lost" or "Monday Mornings" or whatever, we may admire the *way* it was done, but the *what* is a confusing image that leaves us guessing at 'what was worth reproducing.'

The West has only continued to move away from God as the determiner of true beauty and worthy subjects. As a result, our art ceases to convey worthy messages and anyone can now submit any answer to the *what* aspect of the art question. But, perhaps, this is an example of unintentional communication. Maybe there is still a message in our abstract-expressionistic art, only it is not the immediate artist but the ultimate Artist who is speaking to us. Perhaps, God is saying, 'When you rely on yourselves to figure out what's worth reproducing, do not be surprised if you tend to reproduce chaos and confusion instead of breathtaking beauty.'

The Christian and Art

None of this is to say that Christians cannot produce abstract art. It is certainly possible to produce a mystifying work that causes people to say, "This piece speaks to me" in ways that the artist did not even intend. The Christian who has produced such a work might even be amazed by what the viewer/listener takes away from the art. But this can happen with the work of any artist, be they Christian or not.

And so, we must make a distinction between "the Christian's art" and "Christian art." There are several differences that will be helpful to keep in mind.

1. A Christian's art is any work of art that happens to have been produced by a Christian but does not necessarily have to convey a Christian message. On the other hand, 'Christian art' is that which accurately conveys a Christian message, even if it is not produced by a Christian.

   This means that the producer of Christian art is not necessarily a Christian and the producer of non-Christian art is not necessarily non-Christian. It will be helpful to keep in mind too that "non-Christian" does not mean "un-Christian." (more on this in chapter 5)

2. A Christian's art remains dependent upon its human creator for meaning and significance. Whereas, Christian art is dependent upon God/scripture for its meaning and significance.

3. A Christian's art, like the work of any non-Christian is time-sensitive and limited to the life, time and culture of the artist. And even if the art stands the test of time in this world, it will not stand the test of eternity because its subject

matter is earthbound. However, Christian art is produced from an eternal perspective and, because of its subject and message, the relevance of the art will still hold true, even in heaven!

4. A Christian's art may have several interpretations which are equally plausible, and, if interpreted a certain way, could very well be seen as Christian art. But Christian art performs some specifically Christian function and, even without the artist's explanation, speaks for itself and, in doing so, says things which are specifically Christian.

5. If art is an invitation to a cultural discussion about, 'what's worth reproducing?' then every work of art is either a conversation starter, something that advances the discussion, or an attempt to answer the question. A Christian's art can be any one of the three. But 'Christian art' aims to provide a definitive answer to the question, an answer which is grounded in the Christian Scriptures, i.e. the New Testament message.

The confusion with any of this comes when individuals, for whatever reason, begin to demand that a Christian's art always does the job of Christian art. Or, when individuals try to smuggle that which is actually 'Christian art' into the culture as if it is merely 'a Christian's art.' Christians have freedom to do either but, because of the Great Commission, some may feel an obligation to do Christian art. However, I believe that we need both and we Christians who can do both. But, what we really need is Christians who can do both at the same time without denying that either of the two is actually being done.

Ingenuity and Intentionality

If a Christian is determined not to produce Christian art, and yet, still desires to express his Christian heart, he must learn to walk a very fine line between ingenuity and intentionality. It is one thing for the Christian's ingenious artwork to have several different meanings, some on the surface level and some buried deeper; and for the Christian artist to hope that his fans will eventually get all of his intended meanings. It is quite another thing for the Christian artist to be completely unintentional and remove himself from the message-sending process altogether. In that case, it is even more unrealistic for him to hope that the public will walk away having heard his Christian heart and understood his message in any Christian way.

Scripture tells us that, to the pure all things are pure (Titus 1:15). So, a person can get a good or godly message even from a non-Christian's artwork, even if it is an abstract work. Bright colors can brighten someone's day and remind us of the God of all lights; melodious music can cheer the soul and make us thankful for the joy of the Lord. God has rigged human beings as natural interpreters of art and has rigged his world so that everything can serve the purpose of communicating something about him. But it is not to the credit of the artist if he has no intention of communicating in God's favor, what another soul may interpret.

Not just ingenuity but, intentionality, is a must *if* the Christian who is also an artist wants any guarantee that his artwork will communicate something eternally beneficial to his audience. When it comes to these two traits, some art-forms seem to call more for one as opposed to the other. For Christians in the silent arts (e.g. dance, painting, videographers, etc.) ingenuity might seem more necessary since it is often difficult to supply a subtext or explanation that will stand alongside of the artwork. But, again, both are needed.

I am keenly aware of the visual artist's struggle to strike a balance between ingenuity and intentionality. Hardly anyone wants to create works of art with overtly religious scenes just to get the point across. But this is a common temptation and frustration. For instance, when producing music videos, what Christian hasn't wrestled to resist the urge to put a Bible somewhere in the mix in order to visually communicate the message? We struggle to find a happy medium between being so original that our subject becomes unrecognizable and being so predictable, that we become a stereotype.

But those of us who write songs or scripts have an easier and therefore, I believe, more challenging task. We can say whatever we want and explain our point as much as we'd like. And this freedom usually results in either, the beating of dead horses or else, the muzzling of our mouths to the point where we say nothing eternal at all.

The beating of the dead horse occurs when audiences have heard us say the same things so often that they know what we are going to communicate even before the exhibition of our art. They not only know *what* the artist is going to convey but, even worse, they know *how* he is going to convey it. A dose of ingenuity is needed to avoid such un-engaging exhibitions.

On the other hand, the muzzling that occurs happens for one of two reasons: either, as artists, we are afraid that an explicitly Christian message will scare audiences away; or we are bending and catering to that style of art which says 'the more that people have to guess at its meaning, the more artistic the piece is.' The latter is more a matter of art but the former is more a matter of the heart. Whichever one of these reasons has muzzled our message, a dose of intentionality will help us to break through the barriers.

The intentionality that I am talking about can be achieved by a simple task. Sometime before, during or after the creative process (but before exhibition), artists must step outside of their own heads and ask two questions. 1) If I were the viewer/listener and I came across this artwork, what would I be led to believe about any of the following: myself, mankind, love, sex, money, power, good, evil, where we come from, why we exist, the after-life, sin, salvation, Satan, God the Father or Jesus Christ? And 2) Whatever the answer is concerning any of these, can that answer be found or at least grounded in the Bible?

At the very least, if the messages contained in my art concerning any of these topics cannot be found in Scripture, there should not be anything in my production which contradicts what the Bible has to say about these issues. This means that I must take some time to learn what the Bible has to say about them. The Christian heart is a heart that has grabbed a hold of biblical truth and now beats to communicate it. The Christian, who is also an artist, should ask his/herself, "How does this heartbeat express itself as I make a career out of helping people answer the question, 'what's worth reproducing?'"

But be warned. As soon as we begin to formulate our response to this question, another one rises. Specifically: If the Christian's art begins to accurately reflect and reproduce biblical truth and actually becomes that other thing, i.e. 'Christian art,' does it now *have* to be called by that name or can that title be discarded in order to appeal to more people? I will attempt to answer these questions in the next chapter on Branding.

3. BRANDING AND THE BLIND TASTE-TEST

If a Christian's art accomplishes specifically Christian functions, does it have to be called "Christian art?" If calling something "Christian" means that less people will be attracted to it, shouldn't we remove the title in order to attract more people?

Leaving the Christian name off of one's art seems like a logical solution to the problem of people being turned off by our title. And this might actually work, at first. But it will not work for long. In fact, it will eventually begin to work against the artist's mission (the Great Commission) if his art is still accomplishing specifically Christian objectives and yet he maintains that the Christian title does not apply to his art.

Temporarily dropping or changing the name of a product is a marketing move that centers around the concept of branding. Technically, there is nothing wrong with this tactic. But if the Christian desires to engage in this practice, he could learn a great deal from those who have mastered the craft of branding—both biblically and in the world of business. If we look at the issue through these lenses, we will see why taking away the title is only effective when used as a temporary tactic in marketing Christian art.

The Name Game

Have you ever gone into a fast-food restaurant, walked up to the counter and asked for McNuggets, only to realize that you were not at McDonald's? This happens all the time. But what is interesting is, in some cases, the employee who is taking your order will not even attempt to correct you. She knows what you mean and, without missing a beat, serves you her employer's version of chicken nuggets. How does this happen? Simple; it is a matter of excellent branding.

Certain companies, like McDonald's, have done such a great job at branding and marketing their product that we now use their brand-name as if it is the name of the generic thing itself, even though the generic version is made by other companies. This kind of name-brand success can be a blessing or a burden. In this chapter, I will attempt to show why the Christian name has come to be such a burdensome blessing; but a blessing nonetheless. Below, you will find a list of names. Some are brand-names and others are simply the generic names of things that we might use, made by no one in particular. All of the names in the list will have the ® registered trademark logo behind them. But can you identify which ones are actually trademarked brands that are only made by one company?

Ink-pen®
Tooth Picks®
Chap Stick®
Q-tips®
Book-bag®
Jeep®
Walkman®
Motor-cycle®
Pampers®
Vaseline®
Umbrella®
Big Wheel®
Popsicle ®

When you go into a store and ask for any of the above items, are you asking for a specific brand-name or something generic? Even if you end up leaving the store with something generic, when you ask for Chap Stick® Q-tips® Jeep® Walkman® Pampers® Vaseline® Big Wheel® or Popsicle ®, you are asking for a specific brand. There is only one company that makes Q-tips. Everyone else makes cotton swabs. Only one company makes Chap Stick. Everyone else makes lip balm.

But why do we use these brand-names to call for the generic version? Is it because of the branding/marketing team or the quality of the product itself? Or, perhaps, it is due to the fact that the name-branding company was the first one to introduce the item to us. Maybe it is a combination of all three.

But we can ask another interesting question: Is it a good thing or a bad thing when we confuse the popular name-brand with the generic name? The answer depends. It is good for the company if, every time you want generic petroleum jelly, you ask for Vaseline®. That helps to market their brand and increases the chances that you will leave the store with their product. But it is not good for them if you do the reverse. If every time you ask for Vaseline®, you are simply thinking about generic petroleum jelly, then you will leave the store with any brand that meets your budget. Usually, companies do not want their name-branded product confused with the generic.

However, if you ask the makers of the generic brand, you are likely to receive an opposite mixed reaction. It is not good for the generic brands if you, as the shopper, only go the store asking for Chap Stick®. In that case, you are more likely to leave the store with the name-brand product and not the generic. On the other hand, if you as the shopper don't realize that the brand-name is actually a brand; if you think the brand-name is just a generic term, then that is great for companies making the generic product. They know that while you might ask for "chap stick," you will purchase any lip balm you happen to find so long as you like the flavor or the style of the applicator. The generic brand loves being confused with and treated like the name-brand.

But there is a third party we must consider. It is not just the company that created the brand-name or the ones offering the generic version, but the customer who matters. If we were to ask the consumers whether or not they care about the name-brand vs. the generic, the answer will likely be 'no'. If the products function the same way, it makes no difference to the end user what the product is called. Tooth-paste is tooth-paste, unless someone convinces you that Colgate® or Crest® will get your teeth whiter or fight cavities better.

In the same way, when it's all generic: art is art; music is music; religion is religion . . . until someone convinces us that one version functions different from the others; and not just different, but possibly better. You see, everything changes if the brand-name offers some guarantee of quality that the generic brand cannot match. The instant one of the products begins to perform in a unique way the user will automatically characterize and categorize it differently. This happens, not just with name-brands vs. generic brands but, with competing popular brand-names, too.

Just ask morning coffee drinkers about the difference. Try calling Starbucks coffee, 711 coffee, Dunkin' Donuts coffee and McDonald's coffee "all the same thing." Without even getting into blends, devotees of one chain will herald their brand as "real" coffee and all the others as illegitimate, based on the slight, yet noticeable (to them), differences.

God Given Names

Why is it that we demand for things which perform differently to be called by different names? Our minds resist the confusion of using the same name, even when we mean to refer to two things that are similar-but-different. This is not just in the world of business and branding, but even in the biblical world. It seems we have been created to distinguish and categorize things by their unique functions. And then, to give those things distinct names which fit or follow their function.

Go back and look at the creation account in Genesis and you will find that God made a habit of separating things, giving them distinct and different functions, and then naming them based on their unique functions. Consider the following trend from the opening chapters of the Bible:

1. Genesis 1:3,4 God separated, and named Day and Night
2. Genesis 1:6-8 God separated and named the Sky
3. Genesis 1:9,10 God separated and named the Dry Land

4. Genesis 1:14-17 God separated and named the Sun and Moon

5. Genesis 1:26; 2:4,5 God separated man from the ground and named him

6. Genesis 2:19,20 God allows Man to name the separated animal kingdom

7. Genesis 2:18; 21-23 God separated woman out from man and brought her to Adam so that he could name her.

Not far from any of these acts of separation is God's declared function for each separated thing. In fact, if all this were not enough, the very word "created" in the Bible carries with it the sense of being 'cut out' for a purpose. Some scholars even see that the word "bara" translated "create" has its root in the word "to separate." Many of the local peoples surrounding biblical Israel had their own belief systems concerning how the world began. And many of those belief systems involved some story of a deity separating one thing out of another in order to produce the earth. It is no surprise then, that the first words of the Bible tell us that God "created," perhaps, "separated" the heavens and the earth to serve two distinct functions and gave them two distinct names in order to further distinguish them.

If this really is how it all began, then it is clear to see how we, as human beings, psychologically and developmentally, cannot help but to follow this pattern, set by God, as we process the world around us. As toddlers, we incessantly ask the question, "What's this?" We want to know, "What's this thing's function and name?" And we don't stop. We go on to another thing and ask the question again. But once we grasp the answer, we do not go to another thing which looks and functions exactly like the first thing and ask, "What's this?" again. If the left one was a hand, we understand that the one on the right will be a hand as well. If the thin one was a phone, we understand that the thicker one is also a phone.

We may confuse the phone with the T.V. remote control, putting the device up to our ears and pretending to talk. But that is only because we do not yet know that it serves a different function and, is in a separate category of 'thing.' Once we realize it, we stop calling the T.V. controller a phone and go back to asking, "What's this?" because, intuitively, we understand—different function means a separate classification; i.e. a different name. All of this can help us in our discussion concerning how or why Christian art gets labeled.

Some Christians who are also artists complain, "How come in every genre of music, be it country, rock, jazz, classical, rap or R&B, no one else's art has to be labeled religiously, but the Christian's art does?" In tune with this frustration, rap artist Lecrae once deflected the "Christian" title with, "If I'm a 'Christian rapper' then Lupe (Fiasco) is a Muslim rapper." But, aside from the fact that Lupe does not refer to Allah as much as Lecrae refers to Jesus, we will see in a moment that Lupe is still noticeably different enough in his function to get his music labeled differently.

Lecrae's point, however, is still a good one. Lupe and other rappers in that special category they have been lumped into are, nonetheless, much closer to being accepted as 'generic' than Christians are when we say positive things about Jesus over Hip Hop beats, or anywhere in the arts for that matter. Why is that?

Well, it is because all art, if it is not "Christian art," regardless of the form, genre and style, is all accomplishing the same purpose; performing the same function. At best, it is all simply the expert expression and refined reproduction of mankind's unredeemed musings and emotions. "Unredeemed" does not here mean 'sinful.' Rather, it means that the salvation experience is not necessary in order to be able to produce or appreciate the art. This does not make it unproductive. It does, however, keep it in the realm of the generic.

But a Christian's art, if it is Christian art, is designed to do something different. It is not simply expressing mankind's musings and emotion, but God's mind and heart toward man. And even when Christian art is expressing mankind's emotions, it is 'mankind's emotions redeemed.' It is the emotion that a man or woman is only able to have because God the Father has elected, called, drawn, regenerated, given faith to, and began to sanctify the heart of the artist.

When the unsaved general public encounters this kind of art which reproduces something in the salvation experience, they know instantly that something different is happening than what occurs with the usual, generic brand of art. And, it naturally follows that, if the art performs a different function, it deserves a different name. The human brain will demand it! The mind was designed to categorize things in such a way. And it just so happens that the designation that we, in this world, give to things which perform Christianly is . . . well, "Christian."

Interestingly, it is not just with Christian art that this happens. In the Hip Hop world, whenever artists endeavor to perform a different function from the norm, especially if the function is a progressive one, as in the case of Lupe Fiasco, the art is immediately branded as "conscious" or "positive." (Because human nature tends to regress, anything to the contrary will stand out.) At first, in the early 1990's, 'conscious rap' was a proud designation. It stood as the antithesis of the West-coast's gangsta rap. But when East-coast Hip Hop embraced thugism and drugism in the mid to late 90's, conscious rap was buried and ended up underground.

Today, the rappers who are branded "conscious" are often ambivalent about and hesitant to embrace their limiting label. Yet, because they understand the way the human mind works and the role their art aims to serve, these artists accept their "conscious" title and wear it as a badge of honor. This point was expressed by "conscious" rapper Talib Kweli during a 2012 appearance on the *Colbert Report*.

The point is this — the easiest way for a Christian's art to not get branded as "Christian" is for the art to stop doing anything different from what the generic brand is already doing. There are other ways, which we will discuss in the next chapter on methodology. Suffice it to say that it is a blessing that the Christian's heart produces art that serves such a distinct function from the norm. But this distinction and the distinct brand-name it invites is, to some, a very burdensome blessing to have bestowed.

The First Christians

We are not the first generation to fight against being alienated from our culture because of our connection to Christ. The first Christians didn't want to be labeled differently either. The original followers of Jesus were Jews who walked with the Messiah during his earthly ministry. After he ascended and sent his Spirit to be with and in them, to empower and comfort them, the followers of Jesus went back to what they once knew best—the synagogue. But they went back with what they now knew best—the Son of God. And that's when their trouble began.

For those early believers in Jesus, it made perfect sense that they should remain within the realm of Judaism. They saw no need for their new movement to be called by a different name. Of course, there were numerous reasons why they felt this way. Not surprising to anyone would be the relational reasons. The early Christians felt at home amongst their family and friends. They did not want to be rejected by their own people simply for following Christ.

There were also spiritual or theological reasons. In their mind, these Jesus followers were not fusing some newfound, foreign faith together with their former religion. They had grown up with the Old Testament's types and shadows of things to come. And now these men and women were convinced that they had identified the long awaited Messiah. They were only too excited to share with their Jewish brethren how the ancient scriptures had been fulfilled in the life, death and resurrection of Jesus. Lastly, and most interestingly for our current discussion, there was the legal reason for not wanting to be seen as separate and distinct from the established Jewish faith. Judaism had been granted the status of a legal religion in the Roman Empire. This meant that Rome would not interfere with the practice of Judaism and no one saw the religion as a threat to the Pax Romana (the peace of Rome). However, the Romans believed that their peace and safety would indeed be in jeopardy if some of their citizens or subjects began to worship gods who were not on good terms with the rest of the gods in Rome's Pantheon.

At first, the Roman Empire allowed the followers of Jesus to rest under the banner of Judaism. But soon, in Antioch, their differences became too pronounced. The Jews began calling the followers of "The Way" by a new and different name. This new name was necessary because all of their talk about a new covenant and the worship of God who became man proved that "Christians" were going to function differently than what Judaism had been about under the old covenant. Eventually, the Jews complained to Rome that these "Christians" were not about the same thing as the traditional Jewish faith. As a result, Christianity lost its legal status for the next two centuries and periods of intense persecution attended the church.

This was only made worse by the Christians unapologetic assertion that "Jesus is Lord." Remember, this was 1900 years before the dawn of post-modernism so there was no way that these Christians only meant to refer to Jesus' lordship on a personal level; i.e. Jesus is *my* Lord." In the Roman empire, to say that anyone was *your* Lord was the same as saying that that individual *is* Lord. Today, when we make the personal statement Jesus is *my* Lord, it is possible that we are, at the same time, shrinking back from making the universal claim that Jesus *is* Lord. Not so with the early Christians.

Those followers of "The Way" did not call themselves "Christians" first. They only named Jesus as Lord and God. Then, once their society named them "Christian," they accepted it; come what may. In those early days, you could not simply claim the Christian title for yourself. You had to earn it! And many did so by dying for the Gospel. In fact, the test of the true Christian soon became, 'Who is and who is not willing to die because of their connection to Jesus and/or his people?' Call yourself whatever you'd like. But unless you were willing to face death, no one else would bother to call you a real Christian and certainly not a Christian leader.

The Blind Taste-test

But our challenge today (in America, at least) is a little different. We are not dealing with people who disown Jesus in order to keep themselves alive. But, rather, artist detaching the Christian title so that their art, career, or even their efforts in ministry might stay alive. We must ask, is there any wisdom or benefit in this?

In the beginning of this chapter, I talked about brand-names that are so dominant that consumers ask for and end up with the brand, even when they really just want the generic item. What company in the world wouldn't want this type of marketing success? Those who produce Christian art, including Christian rap, have certainly endeavored to build this type of name-brand trustworthiness. But, after coming close to achieving this, what would make an artist or company abandon its brand-name and opt to be classified under a generic label instead?

Well, there actually are a few scenarios which might produce this desire. But none of them are too positive. For example: if a company's product has had bad press; if the product has received a bad review; if some misrepresentation has gone out on the part of the product and public opinion is now so low that the general public is not even interested in giving the product a try; and, if the generic brand is currently in the lead, according to the national consensus—in any of these cases, the company who makes the name-brand would understandably want to do something to either salvage the product's name, or else, abandon the troublesome name in order to blend into the generic market.

For the purpose of this discussion, think of Jesus as the "product" and Christianity as our "brand." This is actually quite accurate, since there are versions of Jesus in other faiths and other world-views. And there are those who include "Jesus" as an inactive ingredient in their mix because they have been allowed to believe that Jesus only desires generic affiliation, not whole-hearted commitment. When we say "Jesus," how do people know that we mean the Jesus of Christianity? It is because of this Christological variety that we ought to be careful before we shed the Christian title, lest we end up endorsing a generic Jesus. We must be clear that when/if we promote his name, that we mean to identify the Jesus of the historic Christian faith.

Now, in many aspects of art, the Christian brand is currently suffering from all of the problems listed above. In light of this, should artists seek to salvage the Christian name or abandon it in order to be branded with the generic label and blend into the general market? We will deal with the second option in the following chapters. Here, let's focus on the mission to salvage and restore the name.

If we were to take this route, two things would have to be true. First, we would have to value all of the work that has gone into the branding process so far. And second, we would have to be convinced that the brand-name has stood and can continue to stand the test of time and, is therefore, worth all the trouble and effort of the salvaging process.

Now, considering all that I have said above about the history of Christianity and how many people have stood and died for Jesus under the Christian brand-name, I don't think that we really want to divorce ourselves from that legacy. So what do companies do when they find themselves in this situation; when they don't want to part with the name of their brand but, rather, salvage it? Some engage in what is known as "the blind taste-test."

In this experiment, a company will put its product up against a competing or generic brand and intentionally hide or remove their own brand-name. Then, if and when the taste-tester gives positive feedback, the company's representative will reveal to the shocked participant that it was such-and-such a name-brand that they have just enjoyed.

I personally think that this is a brilliant strategy which should be employed more often by Christians in the arts. For the sake of this analogy, if Jesus is our product and Christianity is our brand, then the specific art-forms in which we engage would serve as the applicator for the end user or, possibly, the flavor of the product. After the taste-test, we might reveal that the Christian brand of Jesus has just been applied via rap or film or served in the flavor of rap or film. However, if we are going to engage in such an endeavor, we must be mindful that there are at least two things that could easily corrupt the blind taste-test we wish to conduct.

First, what is being offered in the taste-test must represent the truth about the product in question. If the blind taste-tester only likes the product because it has additional features that are not essential to the thing itself, then it is not a true taste-test. Put plainly, Christians must fight the temptation to sweeten the deal by adding un-Christ-like elements to their artistic presentations of Jesus.

I mean, of course taste-testing sinners will want Jesus if he comes with a side of sin; if our presentations are flirtatious, sexy, materialistic, or promise self-centered prosperity and prominence. But how can we do this if the true Jesus demands purity, chastity, marital fidelity, humility, the storing up of treasures in heaven rather than on earth and a heart of servitude?

The second pitfall we must watch out for is blind taste-tests that leave people blind. It would be unproductive for a company to go through all the trouble of arranging the taste-test; to have their product chosen by a participant; but then, thank the taste-tester for her time and send her on her way without revealing to her the name-brand of the product she has just enjoyed.

Or, suppose a particular taste-tester recognizes the brand. This participant has had it before—maybe, never quite like this—but she knows it when she tastes it. She says to the company's rep, "Isn't this such-and-such a brand?" or, put plainly, "Isn't this Christian art?" Only to have the representative, for whatever reasons, swear to her, "No! You're wrong. Don't call it by that name because it's not that brand."

The representative of the company could still go online and tell faithful devotees, "Hey fans of brand-x, guess what. More and more people are choosing the product you know and love. The only thing is, the people who are choosing it, don't really know what they are choosing." But this would defeat the whole point.

The aim is, not just to give people the experience of a taste-test but, to acquaint people with the product and the brand. People need to know where to go if they are to enjoy more than simply a sample. And, in the case of the Christ of Christianity, people also need to know that if they truly partake of the product, then they have become a part of the name-brand that is in desperate need of proper re-presentation.

Jesus > Religion???

This is why campaigns that promote Jesus but not religion are questionable. The popular phrase "Christianity is not a religion, it's a relationship" is not entirely true. It would be more accurate to say that "Christianity is a religion that flows from a relationship." It is, nonetheless, a religion. And the Bible has no problem with that fact.

We, on the other hand, do have a problem with it. We are ashamed of the brand-name "Christianity," and it is understandable to a degree. Consider that, not only have many martyrs died for Jesus in that name but, millions have also been killed or enslaved or oppressed or exploited or intolerably harassed, or persecuted in the name of Christianity. The task of salvaging our brand-name seems too difficult. That is why some people who are a part of the Christian religion mistakenly try to thrust the spotlight and responsibility off of ourselves and back onto Jesus alone, as if he acts without the use of his body—the Church; i.e. the Doctrines and the people (Christians) who make up Christianity.

A close friend of mine struggles to accept Christianity, partly, because he has been hurt by the people of God in the past. But he is quite fond of Jesus. He has a saying which goes, "Jesus, yes; Christians, No!" It is sad that many Christians operate in a similar way. They seem to be saying, "Jesus, yes. Christianity, No!" They say this without taking into account the fact that Jesus is relying on his Spirit working through his people to show the world what "true religion" is, according to the book of James (1:27).

Instead of fighting against our brand-name, we are supposed to be showing the world why this name-brand is to be trusted. We are Christ's body and there is nothing wrong with religion when the body of Christ practices it rightly. But by attacking religion or distancing ourselves from Christianity or the Christian title, we abandon our responsibility and God-given ability to change the way people think about Christianity, Christians and Christian productions and in this case, Christian art.

A better approach would be to band together with the people of God to do something like a reverse of what happened at the Tower of Babel. Our stratified, sanctified subcultures and tongues can now come together, not to make a name for ourselves, but for our great God who has solved our cultural identity crisis and branded us with a new name. The world will know that we belong to him when they see our love for one another and for everyone who bears his brand (John 13:34, 35).

So, when it comes to the arts or life in general, it does not matter whether or not we give ourselves or our art the Christian title upfront. What is more important is, when others take a taste-test and witness our lives or our answers to the question, "what's worth reproducing?" are they forced to characterize our exhibitions as "Christian?" If so, may it be because, like the first Christians, we earned the title due to our distinct function. And, if we earn it, let us not fight against it. Instead, may we wear it proudly; keeping in mind that it is historically un-Christian to choose disassociation with Christ or the Christian name over the loss of life, limb, liberty or limelight.

4. Check the Method

With all this talk about strategy and blind taste-tests, are you saying that there are several viable options for me as an artist who is also passionate about the Great Commission? Or is there only one right way, and a lot of wrong ways, for me to merge my faith and my art?

By now, I'm sure these questions are heavy on the minds of many artists reading this book. It is not my aim to definitively answer these questions for you. However, I would like to lay out several options that will help you to answer these questions for yourself; and also, help you to better understand and evaluate the artistic approaches being taken by others.

When it comes to the arts and the Christian's involvement, I think the choice should be a very clear one. Not necessarily easy to make, but clear to see and understand. To do this, I would like to begin by introducing four clear options for artists. These options are, basically, a matter of matching (or not matching) the Christian *title* to the Christian *function*. And it goes as follows.

The Christian can either: #1 – produce art that aims to accomplish specifically Christian functions and label it as such; #2 – Produce art that amounts to a Christian effort at the end of the day, but seek to not advertise it or brand it as "Christian"; #3 – produce art that is not specifically Christian in function and, also, feel no need to have the Christian label associated with the production; or #4 – produce art that is not necessarily Christian in function and yet, brand and advertise the art as if it is. And so, the four options look something like this:

These four options can be clearly distinguished. The confusion arises, however, when an artist is caught in the progression somewhere between one category and the next, in what I call 'the middle-ground.' As we differentiate between the options, we will be better able to evaluate artistic works as they register at various points along the range of this spectrum. This chapter will focus on options one and two.

Option #1 – Title and Function

Option number one represents artwork which bears the Christian title and, at the same time, is primarily intended to accomplish specifically Christian functions. When artists produce art at this end of the spectrum, they make it known from the outset that they are using their gifts and talents to advance the kingdom of God by evangelizing the lost and edifying the believer.

Specifically, this means the artist has surrendered his art to God to be used as a conduit through which the Holy Spirit can accomplish those tasks which he aims to achieve, primarily, by the use of Christians who are under the Great Commission; i.e.

- convict the world of sin, righteousness and the coming judgment
- call all men to repentance
- be a witness to God's Christ-centered love for the world
- Advertise the salvation that is only possible through faith in Jesus' substitutionary death upon the cross
- be a witness to Jesus' resurrection and his resurrection power

- make disciples while teaching all men what Jesus has already taught
- encourage other believers with spiritual songs and hymns
- exercise spiritual gifts to build up the church
- love the body of Christ with the unique love that Jesus has for his church
- hold other believers accountable to Christ and scripture
- defend the Christian faith
- promote Christ-centered reconciliation
- celebrate marriage as a reflection of Christ and the church
- advocate the raising of children in the fear and admonition of the Lord
- Support the principles of work, relief efforts and mercy ministry to those in need, all as unto the Lord
- Promote the biblical principles of peace, justice, reconciliation and love, primarily among the household of faith to the end that Christians become easily recognizable as Jesus' disciples

While operating within the first option, an individual artistically aims to do any of these things while unashamedly assigning the Christian title to his/her endeavors.

There are obvious benefits and obvious drawbacks to this approach. One benefit is that it identifies and advertises the product to people who are already looking for something that is specifically Christian. These substance-seeking consumers might or might not already be Christians but, it will be helpful for them to be able to easily find what they are looking for.

Another benefit might be that, because it bares the Christian title, the art might be immediately received and find an automatic fan base or market. Indeed, Christian consumers may flock to support the art because they know that, for the most part, they already agree with the content.

There is another benefit, and this point is especially true as it relates to Christian Hip Hop. Christians are often looking for someone to represent us – to prove to the world that we are not corny or out of touch; someone who can give us a way to worship the Savior without making us feel as if we are missing out on the latest trends of culture. The person who can provide this answer becomes a cultural hero to the Christian community (recall the cultural question of heroes from chapter 2).

However, the drawbacks to the approach of performing specifically Christian functions while carrying the Christian title is that, for one, the general public could make two assumptions—one of them true and the other, not so. They might assume that since the art is "Christian art" that it has been produced *by* Christians. This will, in many cases, be true. The other assumption, which is not true, is that the art is only *for* Christians. Some believers have even made this assumption.

But even if the art is laced with the Gospel or biblical imagery, this does not make it for Christians only. For, as Jesus said, "It is not the healthy who need a doctor, but the sick." Christian artists should keep in mind, however, that while they are artistically administering "the cure" it will be helpful to do it with wisdom, love, grace and tact. Just because we have the cure does not mean that we must force-feed it to our patients. We might take a kind of artistic, Hippocratic oath to "do no harm" in our efforts to bring healing to the souls of men and women.

The other drawback to this first option is that it can be spotted a mile away. How does one advertise a cure to sin-sick sinners who love their disease? The Christian title is one of those dominant brand-names which broadcasts things from a distance that an artist may want to wait until she gets close to her audience before she discloses. And most artists know that all of the baggage that comes along with the Christian title could potentially precondition the way their work will be received. The stereotypes about Christians and Christian products include hypocritical, intolerant, close-minded, intellectually thin, and worst of all ("worst," only to some people)—corny.

It is one thing for someone to be "corny" as a rapper or for a movie to be cheesy. It is another thing for people to assume that a rapper is corny or that a movie will be cheesy simply because the Christian label is attached; and then, based on that assumption, either not give the art a chance or not give it a fair chance. The music and film industry also have their assumptions about "Christian art": that it will be too "clean" or G-rated, and consumers will not support it; hence there will be no money in it.

A response to this particular drawback might be that, if a Christian artist can pick up enough steam in the Christian market, the general public will eventually take notice of him and be forced to give a listen. Then the general market will be attracted to the artist or the genre because of the potential sales opportunities. One of the additional functions and benefits of the Christian artist in this case is that, once he gains the ear of the mainstream, he could potentially challenge and change what people think about Christian art, Christian artists, and even Christians as a whole.

That is an exciting possibility. In fact, this is exactly what was beginning to happen with the Christian Hip Hop genre since around the beginning of the new millennium. But, perhaps, for some artists, this ground-gaining was not happening fast enough. This is, possibly, one reason (and there are others) that has led Christian artists to opt for option number two.

Option #2 – No Christian Title, but Christian Functions

Because the hearts of the general public and the charts of the general market are usually closed to explicitly Christian productions, some Christian artists choose to take option number two. Traveling this route, the artist wears no Christian title but still seeks to perform one or several of the Christian functions. This is, in my eyes, not a lesser approach, but definitely a different one. There are a few benefits and a few drawbacks to be mindful of with option number two.

One key benefit is that dropping or never carrying the Christian title might spare an artist from being immediately, professionally marginalized. If the artist can arrive on the scene as uncategorized and generic, she can delay the non-believer's natural negative response to the light that Christians are called to shine. This delayed reaction might allow audiences to pay attention to artwork that they might have, otherwise, rejected before even giving it a chance. And, if they happen to like the Christian function as they experience it, the artist can then reveal that the product was actually a Christian rendition. This is, in effect, the "blind taste-test" mentioned in the previous chapter.

However this approach will only work for so long. The blind taste-test is not designed to last indefinitely. For even if the artist does not ever intend on branding his art as "Christian," once the participant in the taste-test has enjoyed the product, he or she will label it with that title just as long as it is performing specifically Christian functions. When this occurs, the Christian who has produced the art will be faced with an important question: what does he do when his art is consistently branded in this unwanted way by the participants in the taste-test?

This leads to the first drawback of this approach. The drawback is not so much a part of the option itself but, rather, is based in the artist's response to being branded by participants in the taste-test. If the artist has put the weight of his success on his generic-ness, then he might feel the need to tone down the specifically Christian content in his art in order to keep from being name-branded. However, the more he does this, those who partake in his blind taste-test might remain blind when the taste-test is ended. For as we have said, even if the artist mentions Jesus within his artwork, there are other "brands" of Jesus than just the Christian tradition's original rendition.

The second drawback associated with option number two also stems more from the artist's response to being branded than from the option itself. This drawback occurs when the artist who has dropped the Christian title from his art (or never carried it) begins to fight against the title once the public attempts to brand his art with it based on its Christian function.

This adverse reaction sends a confusing message to Christians and non-Christians alike. If it can be clearly perceived that the angle of the art is still very much Christian, and yet the artist is denying that the Christian title applies, believers and nonbelievers might begin to suspect that there is something shameful or undesirable about the name.

As a result, rather than inviting taste-testers to reconsider how they feel about "Christian" productions, the artist who retreats from the title might further encourage audiences to keep their distance from other things which bear the Christian brand (including the Christian community).

But, rather than demonstrating to the world how generic we are willing to become, Jesus had a different idea. If we are going to be addressing issues of faith, we ought not to be speaking from a place of spiritual solitude. Instead, Jesus said that it is by our solidarity with, and love for the people of God that the watching world would know that we are his disciples (John 13:34,35). If this is so, what does it say of our love for the Christian world if we are constantly rejecting the title or issuing disclaimers for things which are truly Christian in nature?

If we understand the connection between the function of a thing and its associated title, the link and progression from option number one to option number two should be clear. Even if we arrive on the scene as artists with no brand-name, once we get branded we do not fight against the title because we know that we perform the function associated with it.

By way of analogy, believers in Jesus in countries where the faith is illegal do not openly brand themselves with the Christian name. This is wisdom. But if someone should happen to corner them and ask the life-threatening question, "Are you a Christian?" They do not deny it and if they do, they feel a world of shame afterwards. Perhaps some of our artists do too when they tell the world they are not making "Christian art."

But let's give the benefit of the doubt that, when Christians in the arts fight against the Christian title, it is not because of shame but, only because of a genuine desire to pull off more blind taste-tests. These artists perceive that they will no longer be able to do so if they allow their art to be branded "Christian." Each artist must examine his/her heart. Whatever the case, this leads artists toward the third option in our chart—no Christian title and no specifically Christian functions. And here is where most of the confusion comes in.

The Middle and the Metaphor

With option number three, there is often debate around the nature of the artwork. Are the productions in this category "Christian art" or simply "a Christian's art?" Before we answer this, or deal strictly with the third position, we must understand something about the progression from option number two to number three. Usually, it doesn't begin in confusion. Yet, sadly, it often ends there.

Innocently enough, the process normally begins when an artist in option number two is set on reaching non-Christians with her art, but sees that her productions are being branded with the Christian title by others a little more than she desires. Perhaps it is because she began her career in option number one and once branded herself this way. Or, maybe it is because of her strong Christian function. No matter which, she cannot pull off many blind taste-tests if the general public already knows that her product is of the Christian brand.

To address this issue, she might attempt to lessen the amount of Christian functions being accomplished in some of her works. And, to balance this out, she might also increase the amount of specific Christian functions she aims to achieve in other artistic pieces. This is a simply a matter of strategy; picking and choosing when she will use her art as a conversation starter with the unbelieving world and when she will use it to clearly convey the redemptive point of her side of the conversation.

But, more and more, as the artist reveals the underlying philosophy/theology behind her substance, she and her art will eventually be branded "Christian" and she must live with the results of the blind taste-test she has conducted. The good thing in this case is that, once branded, she is free to feed her fans without any further pretense. If she chooses, she could confide in her Christian and non-Christian fan-base and say, "Listen, I don't *just* do Christian art. But because I am a Christian, my art will always be a Christian's art." If she takes the time to explain what this means, this would free her up to honesty produce in both categories.

But suppose the artist wants to continue to conduct more blind taste-tests? To do this she would need to continue to conceal her Christian identity. How could she possibly maintain such spiritual secrecy, and yet, still artistically address the spiritual issues beating on her Christian heart? She cannot move all the way into option number three because she is committed to accomplishing specifically Christian functions. This is a serious dilemma for many artists. So what can they do? They can move to the middle-ground between option number two and number three.

This middle-ground is where artists transition into solely using their art as a conversation starter with unbelievers on the subjects of morality and meaning; basically focusing on the "values" and some of the "ultimate questions" from our breakdown of culture in chapter one. And as artists venture into this territory, they understand that they must start and carry on these conversations without bringing the full force of the Christian's side of the discussion to bear convincingly or consistently on their art.

But how can this be done? For starters, an artist might introduce Christian ideas in the form of questions that need to be answered. Indeed, there is a skill to artistically guiding the conversation, be it in music or movies, so that listeners/viewers leave the experience asking the questions and seeking those answers which can only be found within the framework of the Christian worldview.

But, perhaps, there is a way to do more than simply produce art which leaves the audience asking the right questions. There might also be a way for artists to answer those ultimate questions while, at the same time, retaining the spiritual anonymity needed in order to set up more blind taste-tests in the future. For this to happen, an artist would have to disguise the Christian answers in her art to be able to preach without preaching. I believe that this is not only possible but necessary.

What could we gain from having Christians in the entertainment industry and artistic community who are skilled at this form of coded communication? For one, it would give other Christians something to work with as they engage in dialogue with the unbelieving world around them. Just think about it. Who hasn't tried to pour Christian themes into movies like *The Matrix*, *Inception* and *The Lion King* in attempts to share the faith with co-workers, family members, small groups and friends?

Imagine if we had more Christians intentionally producing this kind of art which progressed towards the third option but wasn't quite yet there. In this method, not only is the Christian title removed but the function is disguised. Because of the guise, the artist runs the risk of the general public not being able to perceive the Christian function at all. Many might, therefore, walk away from the artwork having received an unintended message. But, at least, the Christian function is still there, buried beneath the surface and can easily be explained by another believer who, perhaps, works on the same job or lives on the same street as the non-believer who has recently heard the song or seen the movie containing the coded Christian message.

This would put the artwork somewhere in the middle, around here:

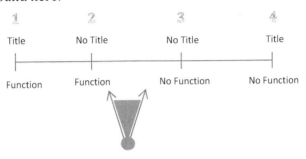

This is beyond the blind taste-test of option number two because, at this stage, the artist is not planning on revealing the brand-name at the end of the exhibition. It is left up to others to come along and help make the connection to the Christian brand. And yet, this approach is not quite all the way over in the category of option number three because there is still some intentional level of Christian functioning at work within the art.

Artists who take this approach should make sure that they are gifted, feel called and can be effective in it. And, also, that they are not taking this route simply because they are ashamed of being publically associated with the Christian brand-name.

If, after taking time for a bit of self-assessment and soul-searching, this is what the Christian artist intends to do, she can very cleverly and creatively design her art around specifically Christian ideas and functions. And to disguise these Christian distinctions, she will likely bury them deep within her art by tucking them inside of a powerful metaphor.

In order to create strong metaphors, one must know both sides of the equation: the subject and the comparison. If I begin by stating that, "Females (the subject) are like flowers (the comparison)," the end of this simile has much more potential meaning if I know a good deal about both females and flowers.

If I know just a little about the subject, I might coin a catchy quote. If I know a little more about the comparison, I might produce a creative metaphorical stanza. However, if I know a great deal about both females and flowers, I could write an entire allegorical script on the concept to powerfully convey my point without ever overtly revealing the subject of my metaphor.

All of this is to say that, as artists in the middle-ground, if we do not have a good grasp on both the Christian faith (our subject) and the culture we aim to communicate the Gospel to (the culture is where we get our comparisons from), we will produce weak metaphors and therefore, mediocre art as we fail to accurately reproduce that which is truly worthy of accurate reproduction.

Common Grace and Hope

If an artist does have a good understanding of the Christian faith, he can do a great deal to communicate both metaphorically and allegorically. But some artists move past this point, heading even further towards option number three (no title and no function), but not quite yet there. These individuals also disguise their Christian function but they do not do it through strong metaphors. They do it by finding common ground with the unbelieving world. And they spend a lot of time in the areas of "common grace."

Common Grace covers all of the aspects of life in which believers and nonbelievers can expect the same degree of care from God, our common creator. Since nonbelievers experience the blessing of necessities like rain and sunlight, the depth of a mother's love for her child, and so much more without ever having to acknowledge God's goodness; the believer can speak on these good things and secretly mean to thank God without the unbeliever ever knowing the godly gratitude behind the art.

And so, in an effort to function in a way that will keep his art from being labeled "Christian," an artist will search the physical and metaphysical world trying to find things that Christians and non-Christians have in common. And in doing this, he will find that it is not just common blessing that we share, but we also share a common hope of better things to come—not merely material things or, even necessarily, spiritual things; just better earthly things, such as real personal and social improvement.

So: wanting a good life; having a desire to alleviate suffering in the world and end hunger or poverty; stopping the violence in the inner-city; ending war in the world; and even the desire to have a life of meaning: the desire for any or all of these things is something that believers and non-believers can share. A Christian artist can voice his hope concerning all of these issues without having to reveal his specific Christian function.

But this is where the real confusion comes in. Notice that I said a Christian artist can speak on these common issues without having to *reveal* his Christian function. Meaning, the Christian function is still there, only the believer is masking it behind the concept of "hope." For, though he is outwardly using generic terms and making religiously neutral comments, in his heart, the believer is actually meaning to convey spiritual realities. In fact, at this point, the artist will likely begin to use "hope" as a generic code-word that serves as a substitute for every spiritual idea he wishes he could openly convey.

When addressing a Christian crowd, the artist will gladly explain the deeper spiritual meaning of the seemingly generic messages conveyed within his art. And, even when creating his art, or presenting it to the non-believing world, he is tempted to illustrate Jesus as the solution to inner-city violence or human trafficking or whatever the social ill. But, if he is disciplined and committed to his cause of finding and holding that common ground with his non-Christian audience, he will not break.

What he might do, however, is search to find more interesting and spiritually significant things that he shares in common with non-believers. Anything that falls in this category will allow him to express his Christian heart and accomplish Christian functions without having to reveal his true intentions. He cannot reveal them because, if he does, he will certainly end up getting himself or his art labeled as "Christian" and this, he fears, will be the end of his blind taste-tests.

Lecrae Moore – A case study

Formerly-known-as Christian rapper Lecrae Moore has even taken it up a notch and done something brilliant. In an effort to still perform Christian functions without being branded "Christian" by the non-believing world, the artist found a very interesting area in which he and his newly acquired main-stream audience could share common ground.

On the *Church Clothes* mixtape, Lecrae voiced a certain kind of disgust or discontentment with the church. Many of his listeners could identify with this. But, unbeknownst to them, Lecrae was only talking about the local church when it operates incorrectly; not the universal church, of which many of his mainstream listeners knew anything about. Walking on this common ground, Lecrae even shared the non-believers hope/fear, "There better not be no *real* church . . . . because that might mean [my] life [has to] change." This, I believe, is a very effective "common ground" approach to garnering unsaved listeners in order to have them hear and begin to consider the Christian world view. It is the tactic of the "Sheep in Wolf's Clothing."

But, as it turned out, Lecrae only flirted with this "common grace" option. He was not willing to simply identify with the non-believer's critique of the church and hope for something better. He went further to reveal the source of his hope. This is key because, as Christians, while we may talk about "hope" along with non-believers, we must always remember that, ultimately, we do not have the same hope as they.

The writer of the book of Hebrews has informed us that our Faith is the substance of the things we hope for. Therefore, it is misleading for Christians to give non-Christians the impression that we have the same generic hope, or that our hope has the same generic basis as theirs—namely, God's common grace. On the contrary, our hope is anchored and name-branded by our Faith in a very uncommon display of God's grace in the person of Jesus Christ. We do not simply offer hope; we offer its substance — faith. And not any faith, but the Christian Faith.

This is why it seemed, to many, unfortunate in 2012 when Lecrae deemed it necessary to argue against the Christian title. Originally, Lecrae was known for employing option number one (Christian title and Christian function). However, it seemed that he had grown a desire to employ option number two—the blind taste-test. This is clearly seen in the fact that, even after dropping the Christian title, the artist continued to accomplish specifically Christian functions through much of his art.

But because of those functions, and because Lecrae had only risen to so high a height due to his success with option number one, it would be almost impossible for him to pull off a blind taste-test. Impossible unless he could, somehow, shake free from the Christian title in the eyes of the general public and the general market.

But this is easier said than done. In February of 2013, well into Lecrae's attempt to shed his Christian title, PBS aired a special feature on the artist and couldn't help but to label him a "Christian Hip Hop artist." In the same month, Lecrae won a Grammy award for Best Gospel Album (the first rapper to do so), even as he continually tried to recategorize himself to each interviewer at the event. His response came, "Technically I'm a Hip Hop artist."

In all actuality, the only way for someone in Lecrae's position to truly get away from the title is to completely abandon the Christian functions and fully engage in option number three—no Christian title *and* no Christian function. But, instead of engaging in option three, Lecrae only began to consistently argue for his right to do so, while dividing his musical offerings between option number two and the middle-ground of common grace.

By disavowing the Christian title, he hopes to completely break out of the box and change the expectation that is placed on his art. Through this, and other means, Lecrae has advanced his career and exponentially expanded his fan-base. Because the Christian functions are still present in his music, other thoughtful Christians can play a part and come behind his efforts, be it through social media or otherwise, and help to reel in the catch of souls the artist has gone fishing for.

But for all of the good that has come, there are just a few cautions that must be mentioned concerning this method of **a)** operating in option two and the middle-ground of common grace while **b)** denying that the Christian title fits and **c)** claiming to simply be doing "honest music" and not "Christian music" as Lecrae does:

1. By denying that the Christian title fits his art when it actually does, the artist's music might be honest but he himself is not being entirely truthful. By continuing to proselytize via his art and build a case for his faith in Christ, his art is, without a doubt, still performing specifically Christian functions and will continue to do so long after he is gone.

2. If what Lecrae is doing is "not Christian" simply because he is willing to say, "it's not," then other artists who own up to the Christian title will be deemed fanatical and overboard; even if, musically, they are essentially doing the same thing as the artist. This is precisely the view that was espoused in a XXL magazine article which featured Lecrae and compared him to Christian Hip Hop efforts of the past.

3. To permanently rip the Christian title from our art (when it actually fits) introduces confusion or contradiction to whatever Christian functions we aim to accomplish. When discussing the issue of tongues in the church, especially in the presence of unbelievers, Paul stressed the need for interpretation and clear communication saying, "If the trumpet makes an unclear sound, will anyone prepare for battle?" (1 Corinthians 14:8)

In the same way, secular media outlets often comment that the good thing about Lecrae's new approach is that it is no longer "too preachy" like Christian Hip Hop of the past. But, in actuality, the artist has not really changed a great deal about his music. What has really changed is the progressive lack of clarity in the way he represents his art. He may still rap about his faith, but he does so with the disclaimer, "Don't worry; I'm a Christian, my art is not."

As Christian listeners, we still like the music because we hear the Christian content and agree. On the other hand, non-believers hear the same content but can now remain undisturbed. By reassuring his audience that he is "not here to preach a sermon," Lecrae has not changed what he does, but rather how his mainstream audience should receive it. They can rest because he is not making Christian professions; he is only offering a

Christian's confessions. But Hip Hop culture has long embraced the idea that 'rappers are preachers.' If this is so, how much more a Christian who raps about life from a Christian perspective?

Things which are Christian have a degree of exclusivity to them and, also, because they promote the claims of Christ, things which are Christian demand a response. Jesus said that he did not come to bring peace but a sword, i.e. division. There is no way to escape having to make a choice. As artists, we cannot allow Christian truths, or our art which contains them, to fall completely into the category of postmodern, subjective truth which only comfortably confesses, "Jesus is *my* Lord" and retreats from professing the universal claim that "Jesus *is* Lord."

When artists fall victim to this, and yet continue to make bold Christian statements (as Lecrae does), these bold statement begin to lose their teeth; no longer gnawing but now harmlessly gumming on the conscious of the unbelieving world while robbing them of the spiritual confrontation with Jesus' universal claims of lordship.

This is indeed the danger of meeting the world's standard of not being "too preachy" by removing/denying the Christian title. Even though what Lecrae means to convey is "You don't *have to be* a Christian to listen to/like my music." What he runs the risk of communicating is "You don't *have to become* one either." The more artists argue for a general branding and treatment of their art, the more their Christian content will become relegated to realm of the generic as well.

4. By removing the "Christian" title while still using specifically Christian terminology, we give license for others to use the same terminology but in generic ways. In 2004, Kanye West released his hit song "Jesus Walks." In it, he talked about paying for his sins by making the sacrifice of producing the song about Jesus which might have cost him radio pay.

   Though this sacrifice is noteworthy, the idea was nonetheless erroneous. However, seven years later, in 2011, he was still under the same belief that this generic association was sufficient. On "OTIS" he rapped in reflection, "I made 'Jesus Walks' so I'm never going to hell." In 2013, pseudo conscious rapper, Kendrick Lamar rapped about buying a Bible after making his 1st million dollars. He confidently exclaims, "Yeeeah, God got me."

Several verses later he reveals what he was able to do with his next million and how the success and fame that God secured for him now enables him to have illicit sexual encounters with his listener's favorite female singers. And this is after being green-lit by Lecrae on many occasions. And, also, after Lecrae had consistently argued for his own artistic generic-ness.

As artists, we must be sure that the truth in our message is never allowed to be downgraded to generic or, that we do not help the perception that the generic-ness of others has been upgraded and now serves the same function as the old "Christian" brand.

5. By denying that the Christian title fits his art, the artist has disconnected himself from and cast shade on an entire genre which

   a. served as the springboard for his own entrance into the spotlight.

   b. is not just a genre but a counter-culture that houses the very people who will likely be key in helping to disciple those who might come closer to Jesus through Lecrae's "non-Christian" music.

With comments in interviews such as "90% of Christians who did rap in the past were terrible," Lecrae does little to improve the name-brand for those who are still laboring within the Christian

Hip Hop counter-culture. Rather than improve the world's perception of Christian Hip Hop, he has separated himself from it while he further promotes the same misconception that he hates for other people to place on his own faith-based art before they hear it.

This misconception ignores several important factors such as; some Christian rappers may have limited themselves to only seeking musical production from other Christians who, unfortunately, may not have the 'name' or new sound or current technology. They do this, not because they are addicted to mediocrity but, because they have determined not to lean on the strength of well-known secular producers and end up owing their success to them instead of strictly to the glory of God. On top of this, there is very little financial backing or industry (secular or Christian) support for Christian rap music.

Lastly, even if Lecrae's 90% figure is accurate and not exaggerated, it could be argued that, with so many people endeavoring to rap these days, the majority of rappers in every category, not just Christians, are terrible. It just so happens to be that generic rap gets more light shown on its 10% of "good" artists, meanwhile the Christian community's percentage of good artist (the figure is no doubt higher than only 10%) is simply more underground than even conscious rap.

6. Lecrae's current strategy cannot be employed by any and every one. Young artists who watch him might assume that the key to general market acceptance is to, like him, simply do spiritually "honest music" without calling it "Christian." This is attractive because Lecrae is still able to pack a good deal of Christian content into his art. However, this only works because Lecrae was already well known as a Christian artist. It will be virtually impossible for an unknown artist to include as much Christian content as Lecrae currently does while attempting to brand oneself as "not a Christian artist."

If the content is there, the name will come. Now, an artist may choose to fight it but we see just how difficult of a task that is, even for Lecrae still. With Christian functions in the art-form, it is only possible to begin separating the title once an artist has built up enough success and momentum (as a Christian artist) that people want to hear from him no matter what he calls himself because they have grown to trust the consistency of his art and message.

But realistically, if you are packing Christian messages, you will need the Christian market/fan-base. Even Lecrae was not able to reach this level without them, as his Christian fan-base with their purchasing dollars is what made Lecrae attractive to the general market.

Freedom to Move

It is extremely difficult, after beginning one's career in option number one and experiencing success, to move towards the middle-ground of common-grace, and to retain the ability to perform option number two. This is the marvel of what Lecrae has done, or is currently attempting to do. In some ways, it is easier to begin without the Christian functions or the title, in option number three and then to move toward option number two. But there are just as many cautions when traveling that direction. However, this does not mean that it is not a worthwhile pursuit and some artists might want to consider it, especially if they are not already well known.

However, if Lecrae's art really did register as "not Christian art" with no title and no specifically Christian functions, one wonders what type of support he would receive from the Christian community. But we will see that, if an artist chooses, he has every right to travel that route and can do so without having sinned one bit. And there are many Christians whose art, both audio and visual, registers in the range of the third position in our spectrum.

So, now that we have seen something of the progression from option number two on into the middle-ground, we can turn our attention to look specifically at the third category and what it has to offer. As with options one and two, in the next chapter, I will lay out the benefits and drawbacks of Christians producing art that has neither the Christian title nor performs any specifically Christian functions.

5. NO TITLE AND NO FUNCTION

Can't I produce art that does not accomplish any specifically Christian function? Aren't there other things in life that are worthy of reproduction outside of what is summed up in the Christian's mission? Can't I just do art as my 9 to 5 job, or my personal hobby and use other areas of my life to respond to the Great Commission?

In the previous chapter, I introduced the four popular directions in which Christian art tends to go. Here, I'd like to discuss the common motivating factors that lead some Christians to choose option number three—No Christian title and no specifically Christian function. Also, as with the first two options, we will look at the benefits and drawbacks of this approach.

Look again at the list of options in the Christian art spectrum. The highlighted portion is what I call "the sweet spot."

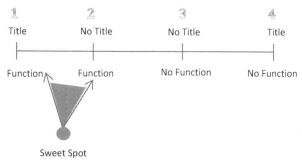

Sweet Spot

Many Christians, who are also artists, want to produce art that registers somewhere within this range on the chart. They'd like it if their productions could be marketed to Christians as "Christian art" but, also, if their work could be presented to the general public without that title or, simply as "a Christian's art." We have covered some of the reasons why a person might desire this duality in the previous chapters. But there are three concerns in particular that lead artists to the doorstep of option number three.

1. *Genuine Common Grace Interest*

The first concern is a sincere interest in the areas of common grace. Common grace subjects are not just good for disguising specifically Christian functions. They are real areas of life in which Christians exist and, understandably, might desire to artistically express themselves. Christians can experience romantic love, heart ache, heart break, big dreams, crushed dreams, the simple pleasures of life, good days, bad days and so many other common human experiences.

It is true, biblically speaking, that the Christian has access to extraordinary insight into these ordinary events. But there is no law which states that Christians have to bring their eternal perspective to bear upon their art, effectively turning it into 'Christian art.' If the believer chooses not to do this, the end product can still be referred to as 'a Christian's art,' and might have several benefits which we will discuss below.

2. *Christian = Predictable*

The second concern that motivates artists to choose the option of 'no Christian title and no Christian function' is the general public's preconceived notions about "Christian art." Many Christians, who are also artists, fear that when other people hear the term "Christian" they think, "I already know what it's going to sound/look/be like and what it's going to be about."

3. *Predictable = Inartistic*

The third concern is based on the second; that is, that there is something inartistic about art that does not inspire a sense of wonder. Or that the art will come across as un-engaging if it does not cause the viewer/listener to ask existential questions about the piece, such as, 'What was the artist really *trying* to say?'

If the viewer/listener can just about assume or predict everything the artist is going to attempt to convey, all at first glance or upon first listen; or, even before witnessing the artistic piece, then there was really no need for the exhibition of the art. However, if the artist can capture a certain sense of mystique, then the experience will seem all the more artistic. This is an attempt to appeal to the "sophisticated" minds of the descendants of the Enlightenment (which we all are culturally speaking).

Why the Third Option

When dealing with the unbelieving, skeptical and even hostile person, options number one and two have their place in the Christian's mission. But, often, these methods are straight forward and don't leave much room for imagination. Hence, the middle-ground (between options two and three) approach of communicating metaphorically may be the most attractive for modern artists because it seems to call for more creativity, less objectivity and presumably, less predictability.

This is appealing in a world where subjectivity has become "sexy" and truth has been exchanged for choice and personal opinion. Even the middle-ground approach of operating in "common grace" is not without its place in the Christian's mission because, though the artist seems to be speaking generically; he, inwardly, means what he is saying in the most Christian way possible.

But, even after all of this, the most a Christian artist can accomplish through these middle-ground tactics is the creation of what I call 'unpredictably-predictable-art.' In the following chart, the creative Christian artist will produce art that registers in the lower left and upper right quadrants:

The Creative Christian Artist

	Ways	Whats
Predictable	Predictable Ways	Predictable Whats
Unpredictable	Unpredictable Ways	Unpredictable Whats

The art is unpredictable in that, we cannot grow comfortable in assuming that we know *how* the artist is going to go about making her point from one work of art to the next. However, the art is predictable in that, if you already know the Bible's message, you will, to some degree, already have some idea and understanding of *what* the artist's message is going to be, even if it takes her a while to get around to it or for audiences to arrive at it.

But it is this very fact—the fact that the audience can safely assume that they will arrive at a Christian message—that makes even the middle-ground approaches unsatisfactory for some Christians who are also artist. These artists move all the way into option number three and will even look to reverse the way they are categorized. They will demand, instead, to be referred to as "Artists who are also Christians" because they see themselves primarily as artists. The "Christian" part is not necessarily an aspect of their professional identity and, therefore, we should not expect to see any specifically Christian functions at work within their productions.

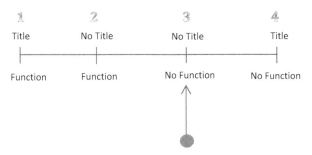

This approach goes beyond the middle-ground of "common grace" because, here, the artist is not secretly trying to also convey a "Christian" theme and there is no intended way to spin the art so as to end up with a redemptive message.

Remember, to entertain means to cause one to focus on a fixed point or subject. And, related to it, the artistic question is, 'Was this' or 'Why was this subject worth reproducing and fixing our gaze upon?' In options one and two, artists tend to do a better job answering this question than they do of causing their audiences to ask it in the first place.

In the third category, the reverse is often true. It is not the artist's answer that matters but, rather, how deeply the artist can cause the audience to ask the question. And, even if an answer to this question is offered within the frame of the artwork, it is not a biblically grounded answer but, rather, a debatable one which is left to be settled in the soul of each viewer/listener, or the community in which they live.

Therefore, the artist taking this approach can touch on pain, misery, meaninglessness, lust, hope, suffering, relief, victory, love, loss, betrayal or any number of themes without ever giving a biblically accurate commentary on whether or not the subject was worth reproducing in the way it has been portrayed within his art. And, without any such objective source or stance, his art is no longer a conversation starter with the unbelieving world. It is now a full fledge conversation piece with no definitive or final statement. It is still a conversation about the cultural questions of art, but the conversation remains open-ended precisely because the Bible has remained closed.

The closed Bible (and silencing of the biblical world view) effectively does away with the problem of predictability. If true artistry is the expression of the soul, then a true artist cannot be "put into a box," pigeon-held or limited to a certain expression; not only a certain form of expression (*ways*), but limited to the expression of certain distinct functions (*whats*). Artists operating in the third category will look to produce art which registers in the lower left and lower right quadrants of *Ways and Whats's* chart:

Creative Artists, who are also Christians

	Ways	Whats
Predictable	Predictable Ways	Predictable Whats
Unpredictable	Unpredictable Ways	Unpredictable Whats

Without the Christian title to limit them, or any commitment to accomplishing specifically Christian functions, there is no longer any way to box these artists in. They are now free to produce "regular art" with no external expectations; bound only by the limitations of their own abilities and consciences.

For reasons that will be discussed below, it is not uncommon for artists who choose option number one (Christian title and Christian function) to be suspect of those who operate in option number three. Likewise, artists who take this third approach have shown their contempt for artists who prefer the more overt method of option number one. And during these debates, artists in the range of option number two find themselves caught in the middle, perhaps, because they have preferred the middle-ground.

Modern-day Daniels?

Must there be such an adversarial relationship between the artists in these various categories? If we were to give them all the benefit of the doubt, there is a way to view this issue which might be helpful to all parties involved. To borrow militaristic terminology, we could compare the artists in each category to soldiers fighting on the same side, but on different fronts in the same war.

Those who take option number one (title and function) have chosen the full frontal assault, arriving under fierce fire on the heavily defended shores of the unbelieving heart and mind. Those who take option number two (Function but no title) are engaged in the subtle attempt to flank the opposing forces from the side. Those taking the middle-ground of metaphor and common grace have parachuted over all of our heads or tunneled underground to come in through the backdoor and surprise the unbelieving world.

But option number three (no title and no function) is like planting secret agents in the "enemy's" camp. These agents might serve for years as "sleeper cells" until they are activated. And, until then, these artists live normal lives, doing normal things and working regular jobs like everyone else around them. Their art is merely their job. These artists would compare themselves and their role to the biblical prophet Daniel who, literally worked in his enemy's camp. But there are several things we must keep in mind when making this comparison:

1. *Daniel did not choose his situation; rather, he was chosen.*

   Daniel's life and circumstance occurred during a time when his people were captives in Babylon. During that captivity, Daniel, through no fault or choice of his own was in a foreign land and selected to be groomed to serve the Babylonian king. He became a servant in that regime; a regime that did not recognize his God. His only choice in the matter was to honor his God in the midst of it all.

   And yet, this was possible because Daniel's captor was an instrument in the hand of God. King Nebuchadnezzar was a secular ruler whom God used to serve a sanctified purpose in his plan for Israel (namely chastisement). Can this be compared to our modern circumstances today where we, for the most part, get to choose where our talents will be employed? Perhaps.

   Since toilsome labor is an inescapable part of the curse which we all live under as sin's captives, we could possibly compare our "daily grind" to Daniel's dilemma. But the lesson to learn from his scenario is not 'how to remain spiritually undetected in order to launch sneak attacks while excelling professionally in a secular world.' Rather, it is, 'how to use life's unavoidable, necessary evils for spiritual good, at the risk of *not* professionally excelling in a secular world.

2. *It is precisely because Daniel took risks for the sake of his faith, not because he played it socially safe, that his story is recorded in Scripture.*

   Daniel's faith played a major role in his life. In fact, it is because of his faithfulness that God ensured Daniel's advancement in Babylon. But, until the key moments when Daniel's faith became an undeniable factor, in the eyes of the unbelieving world around him, Daniel seemed to maintain his professional position simply by excellently doing the same mundane jobs as anyone else in the "enemy's" camp. And he was willing to do so unless or until he was asked to deny or defy the Living God.

   Many Christians who take the third option argue that they are doing no more and no less than the prophet. If ever the right moment comes along, these artists will proudly throw their lot in with the people of God and make a stand for their faith. But, it would have to be a pretty big moment, indeed, for them to "blow their cover" and reveal their committed Christian hand. Until then, they are relying on their excellence in craft to win for them the favor and position which will make their future declarations of faith all the more noteworthy.

However, artists in this category must keep in mind that it is not merely the future, "someday" declarations of the Daniel type which matter, but the earlier ones as well. Daniel's later declarations were only possible because of the social risks he took as a young man when he chose to stand for purity and worship God alone, even if it costs him his life!

3. *Daniel was committed to Godly purity, not simply purity for purity's sake.*

It is tempting for artist in the third category to tout their strong morals in the midst of a secular society as proof of their role as modern-day-Daniels. But Daniel had more than this in mind. When he made his petition not to defile himself with the king's food, it was clear to his captors that his concerns were not dietary but in light of his deity.

When artists, who are also Christians, miss or fail to communicate this point concerning Godly purity, they end up with a different label—not that of "Christian" but, rather, simply "conscious," "positive" or "clean-cut." Like the popular Christmas song, their goodness is seen as being "for goodness sake" not for God's sake. They will be amalgamated into the category of the conscious artist.

This branding is actually ideal for some artists in the third category. They are hoping that the moral-but-not-necessarily-spiritual stances they hold might gain for them a voice in the current conversations; a seat at the round table as their input is sought on the social discussions of the day; be it on gun control, free speech, rights to marry, or what have you.

These artists, who are also Christians, can keep their seat at that table so long as their faith does not take over the conversation. They will end up in front of the cameras when something terrible happens in the culture and moral guidance is needed. This, they feel, is the equivalent of a "Daniel" type.

Daniel was, indeed, sought in times of trouble. And he was excellent in his professional life when not being publically, spiritually active. But he was, nonetheless, consistent in his commitment to his faith and godly purity. So much so, that the only "fault" his enemies could find in him was his dedication to the God of his fathers (Daniel 6:5). Artists who desire to be modern-day Daniels must ask themselves, 'Can it be said that my commitment to God and God's ways are as known by non-believers as my commitment to excellence?' *That* was Daniel.

4. *Lastly, Daniel was not a loner but, instead, had fellowship and accountability from like-minded, even if less-talented, people.*

In Daniel chapters 1 and 2 we learn that, though God had gifted the other "three Hebrew boys," Hananiah, Mishael, and Azariah, Daniel was given abilities above and beyond theirs. Yet this did not stop Daniel from seeking their companionship and spiritual cooperation in his times of need.

Therefore, if artists, who are also Christians, are going to make a career of existing in the secular arena, I believe Daniel would encourage the close knit community and accountability of others who, though they may not be as skilled, are just as committed to the life-mission of glorifying God even at the risk or expense of personal advancement.

Category Mistakes

Daniel was not an "artist." But if we were to compare his function to our discussion, because of his frequent strong stances, it could be argued that he did not operate in option number three, but rather fluctuated between option number two (Function but no title) and the middle-ground of common grace.

I do not want to paint the picture that option number three (No title, no function) is an un-Christian option.

However, it does sometimes come with controversy. One of the reasons for this is, when fans and followers do not fully understand how or why an artist is fluctuating between categories, they might attempt to label an artist's work and keep that artist in a certain category when the artist wants the ability to move freely up and down the spectrum. But another reason is, not infrequently, artists who employ option number three, add to the confusion by misrepresenting their own artistic efforts.

This happens whenever artists in the third category claim for themselves the credit that usually comes from engaging in option number one (Christian title and Christian function) or option two (Christian function but no Christian title) when, in fact, they are not.

There are two common reasons why artists make this questionable claim: either, as far as they know, these artists are operating in the range of options number one and two to the best of their limited ability; or, these artists want the credit, acclaim and Christian support that usually comes with options one and two but without having to make the professional sacrifices that go with the territory. Let's look at both of these.

Charge it to the Head: Living up to what we have obtained
Some artists, who are also Christians in the third category, see no difference between what they are doing and what Christian artists do when they are conducting the blind taste-test. But it is only because these artists do not have as strong a grasp on their faith as they ought

to have, that they cannot distinguish between the two. Since they know their own hearts and what they believe in, they feel their art ought to be accepted *as* Christian *by* Christians, even if they do not make matters of eternity the subject of their production.

I can think of several artists for whom this was the case and one in particular. In the summer of 2008, I went to a Philadelphia bar to show my support for the artist Braille. In many circles, Braille was known as a Christian artist but in others, simply as an artist who was also a Christian. I, among others, often wondered why Braille wanted or needed the Christian title attached to his art which, normally, did not accomplish any specifically Christian functions.

However, that night, I remember watching him perform his new song "Blessed Man" in which he talked about the many things for which he was thankful: divine protection, his family and his relationship with God which was secured through Jesus' cross. Compared to the rest of his then current catalog, this was one of the most explicitly Christian songs I had ever heard from the artist.

I assumed that, in those days, Braille was operating mostly in the third category and, at times, the middle-ground of common grace. And so, I was shocked and excited by this particular song in which he had chosen to, rather uncharacteristically, accomplish specifically Christian functions.

However, several years later, in 2013, Braille informed me that back in those earlier days, he believed that he was operating completely inside of option number one (Christian title and Christian function), not just in the song "Blessed Man," but with his entire discography, earthbound as the content may have been. The problem was, according to him, because his knowledge of the Christian faith was so limited back then, he could not offer to others what he himself did not have.

Scripture instructs us that each man only has the responsibility to live up to that which he has attained (Philippians 3:16). The solution, then, in cases like the 2008 Braille, is not to insensitively demand more faith-filled art from the artist but, rather, prayer that the artist might be filled with more faith. Much like Apollos who preached John's baptism until the Gospel was explained to him, artists in this predicament would, without hesitation, do a better job at executing options number one and two if they had the wherewithal to do so (Acts 18).

Charge it to the Heart: Wanting our cake, and eating it too

But what about the other possible reason for artists who make this category mistake? Do some in the third lane falsely claim to be working in the range of options number one or two simply because of the benefits that come along with those categories? These benefits include the immediate reception from a Christian audience and therefore, the Christian market. This is especially a sore spot if an artist is only schmoozing up to the Christian market because he/she is currently experiencing a slump in the general market or having a hard time picking up steam there.

Another benefit is the potential for these artists to become heroic figures in the eyes of the Christian community. (Recall the role of cultural heroes from chapter one.) This can happen quite easily because the Christian community is too often too desperate for cultural heroes, especially ones that have been accepted and approved by the secular world. As a result, artists in the third category are sometimes welcomed and celebrated by Christians simply for claiming to be Christian or making promises to artistically perform specifically Christian functions; whether or not they ever actually perform them.

This could rub other Christian artists the wrong way because, even though artists operating in option two and the middle-ground of metaphor get to receive Christian artist's benefits without having to bare the Christian title, they do, however, still run the risk of being associated and branded with the title because it can be easily demonstrated that they are actually aiming to accomplish specifically Christian functions.

But artists in the third category unjustifiably reach for these rewards. Their art has no Christian title *and* performs no Christian functions so, for them and their careers, there is no risk. Their claim to Christian artist fame rests in the fact that they themselves are willing to be identified as Christians outside of the realm of the arts. And because they are Christians, they would argue that, regardless of the content of their productions, "A Christian's art can and should receive whatever support and acceptance is usually reserved for Christian art."

However, their position can be easily reversed if these artists sense that they are about to be professionally or artistically handicapped because of their Christian connection. The reversal comes with just a flip of the phrase to, "A Christian's art doesn't always have to be Christian art. So don't put me in that box."

This is the reason why artists in the first category have, in the past, made such a big deal about these inaccurate claims by artists in the third lane. It is partially a matter of fairness and partially an issue of spiritual honesty. Fairness because, artists in the first two categories often have to die to their rights to pursue the spoils that come along with the third category (mass appeal, fame, fortune, glory, etc.) and yet those in the third, without making any such sacrifices, would still claim for themselves what little earthly rewards remain for those operating in options one and two.

This misrepresentation creates a new middle-ground on our options chart, not between numbers two and three but between options three and four, putting artists somewhere around here:

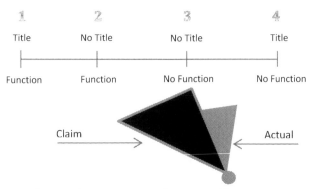

But this is also an issue of spiritual honesty. We might liken it to Ananias and Sapphira in the book of Acts. The (presumably) Christian husband and wife couple sold their property and then went to give some money to the church. But, in the process, they told a deadly lie. They did not have to give all of the money they received for their property to the church. They could have kept some of it or, even, all of it for themselves. But they wanted the honor of being able to say that they had given their all. Their deception came as they reported, "We sold our land and got this much for it. And look, we're giving all of it to the church."

They looked around and waited for the applause of the people. After all, everyone else was giving their all; how could Ananias and Sapphira give any less? But because they had received much more for their land, they actually had much more to give if they were really going to be true to their claim of giving their all. Before pronouncing his judgment on them for lying to the Holy Spirit, the Apostle Peter explained, "When the property was yours, you had the right to do with it as you pleased. And even after you sold it, you could've done whatever you wanted with the money."

In the same way, as artists who are also Christians, we have the right to do whatever we want with our talent (except sin). And we do not have to give it all over to the Great Commission. But, neither do we have the Holy Spirit's permission to lie about how much of it we have given to the Gospel mission after we have kept back some of it for ourselves.

The Benefits & Drawbacks

None of this is to say that when artists, who are also Christians, choose option number three, they are sinning. They are not! In fact, there may be some Christians who, though they could take options number one or two, they feel, however, as if they have been wired to take option three. And others who, may not feel wired to do so but, might be hired to —engaging in option number three strictly for work.

Jesus said, "Out of the abundance of the heart, the mouth speaks." If art is, as we say, an expression of the soul, it is difficult for us to imagine a Christian whose heart and soul does not pump out Christ-centered works every hour of the day. But this difficulty does not mean that such a case is impossible. However, the Christian who feels lead to travel option number three, should be sure that he is not pulled in that direction simply because he is not properly acquainted with the Gospel and biblical principle of Justification by Faith. Frequently, this lack of familiarity with the true gems of the Christian faith has been the reason for artists staying away from options number one and two.

If an artist, who is also a Christian, engages in option number three strictly for work, she has every right to do so but should keep in mind certain cautions as well. If she does a work for hire, and the one who has hired her has not asked to be reminded of biblical truth; so long as the Christian is not knowingly producing a backdrop for sin, she has done nothing wrong. On top of this, there is nothing deceitful about an artist (e.g. a dance choreographer for an upcoming play) in this predicament letting other Christians know about the upcoming production so that they can show their support. At the very least, other Christians can rejoice in the production of clean, quality art that they will not have to endure evil just to enjoy.

But if the artist, who is also a Christian, has any freedom at all, any say over the direction of the art, she should be mindful that there is nothing in this world that cannot quickly become "as unto the Lord." Paul mentioned eating or drinking to the Glory of God. Jesus informed his disciples that if they gave someone a cup of water in his name, they had done it unto him.

So, then, an artist who simply wants to paint a scene from nature can paint that scene to the Glory of God. Especially if she considers that Romans chapter 1, along with Psalm 119, tells us that the creation preaches incessantly about the majesty, power and eternality of God. But even nature tells the story of our need for restoration. "The grass withers and the flower fades because the breath of the LORD blows upon them" (Psalm 40:8). And Romans 8 tells us that all of creation is groaning, complaining as it waits for the coming redemption. This means that nature, in all its beauty and grandeur, is not happy with itself and will not be until the children of God are revealed.

This means that, if we are going to be artists who tell the truth in our art, whether our subject is a nature scene, the animal kingdom, human government, romantic relationships, etc.; the truth about each of these must include, or at least have in view, a groaning anticipation of redemption. It might be that artists in the third category can help serve the Christian mission by expertly depicting the many facets of creation as caught and existing in between the two realities of grandeur and groaning, even if they cannot or will not show specifically what it is that all of creation is groaning for.

But, aside from possibly serving this function, what other benefits might come from artists operating in the third category? We have already alluded to the fact that those who take this option will be met with fewer struggles in their careers. And, we all know that artists already struggle enough as it is.

On top of this, the artist who is also a Christian operating in the third lane, might serve as living proof to his fans that Christians aren't really so bad. If his Christianity is known by the public, he may help to convince the world that we are not all "Bible-thumpers" looking to shove our beliefs down people's throats. By speaking on regular, common grace issues, he will demonstrate that Christians still exist in, take part in and care about all the facets of life that make the human experience so dynamic. (Even artists who operate in option number two could do more of this. It is a shame that Christian art is not known for practically dealing with real life issues.)

Having destroyed the stereotype that the Christian life is all Bibles and baptisms, the artist in option number three will have fans who say things like, "I wish all Christians were like him; *him* I can take." The artist will have to decide whether or not this is really a compliment to his Christianity. But the artist will no doubt prove that Christians are "real people" too with real issues who do regular things.

Another benefit is related to this; artists taking this option might gain a greater platform which will put them in touch with more and more people because their art does not include the exclusive functions of

Christianity. But all of these benefits come with drawbacks that are just as inter-related.

For starters, if, by choosing the third option, an artist gains the acceptance of the general public, this acceptance will be a hard thing to risk losing. It will be especially hard if she has gained this acceptance by seemingly distancing herself from other Christians or Christ himself. Consider Peter, who denied Jesus as he warmed himself around the fire of those who did not believe. In fact, he began to "swear" and call down curses upon himself in order to convince his new associates of the distance between himself and Jesus (Matthew 26:74).

Similarly, artists in the third category are often tempted to rely on profanity, vulgarity, nudity or vanity in order to remain in good standing in secular settings. But we must not grow so comfortable in ungodly communities that we cannot perform our Christian function, both in the opportune times and in the seemingly inopportune times. For we must be instant in season and out of season (2 Timothy 4:2). Our art may be excused from this command, but not we ourselves.

Another drawback associated with this option is that, artists in the third category (and their Christian fans) might begin to believe that being "in touch" with more people is the same thing as "reaching" more people. We are "in touch" with people when they know about us and know where to go in order to get our products; when they tweet about us and like us on Facebook. But we have only "reached" them when we have performed for them some specifically Christian function without, at the same time, sending un-Christian messages that nullify the functions we aim to accomplish (Revelation 3:15; 1 Corinthians 14:8).

But, even when we have reached our desired audience, we must keep this one thing in mind. After we strategize and come up with ways to get in front of millions of people, if we, at that point, choose to seize the moment for the Gospel; still, the chosen are few. Yes, those who believe will be saved. And people cannot believe in one they have not heard of; and they cannot hear without a preacher; and preachers will not go unless they are sent. Still, redemption of the nonbelieving world is not rooted in our ability to call many more people unto salvation.

We may call as many as is humanly possible. But Jesus warned that, even of the many who respond to the massive call, some will be turned away they have not come to be clothed in the righteousness of Christ (Matthew 22:1-14). They only came to have their temporary (emotional, intellectual, social) needs met, which the Christian's art may be good for. But they did not come to have their eternal needs met, a task for which Christian art exists to accomplish (John 6:26, 27). And no one can come to Jesus correctly unless they are drawn by the Father (John 14:6). We are the instruments through which he calls. But, in the end, it is he who calls, he who draws and he who chooses.

It is also he who will reward each one of us, including, each artists, according to what we have done in his name. Therefore, who are we to judge another man's servant (Romans 14:4)? Only let each servant/artist be mindful that we will all have to give an account to our Lord. May we therefore serve him all the more faithfully; knowing that he is soon to return and his reward is with him (Romans 2:6; Jeremiah 17:9, 10; Matthew 25:14-30).

6. CHRISTIAN MUSIC AND THE GOSPEL-LESS GOSPEL

Since Gospel literally means 'good news', is there only one specific 'good news' message that Gospel artists must proclaim or can any good news whatsoever qualify as Gospel?

In the last chapter I brought up the subject of artists in the middle-ground between the third and fourth category who do not want the Christian title nor want to perform specifically Christian functions, but who wish to still receive some of the benefits that come to those who do. In this chapter we will look at the fourth option where, artists happily apply the Christian or Gospel title to works which do not perform a Christian function or carry the Good News of Jesus Christ.

Some will dispute the content of this chapter by saying that my concerns here are merely theological or doctrinal; that we are free to agree to disagree; and that none need be bothered if I happen to touch a nerve or hit too close to home with this topic. "Christianity is more than just doctrine," they'd say. To which I would agree. But I would add, in the words of Pastor Many Ortiz, "Christianity is much more than doctrine; but it is also not less than doctrine."

And so, with this admonition in mind, I'd like to discuss the three most common forms of art which bear the Christian title but do not perform Christian functions. They are, that which teaches merely moralism instead of justification; that which preaches the Old Covenant instead of the New; and that which celebrates deliverance over and above salvation. The first of these is not religious at all. The remaining two are called "Christian" but are, in fact, **pre-Christian** in their message. All of these register at the far end of the spectrum.

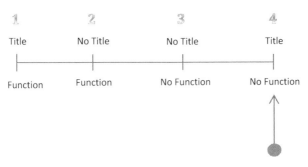

Merely Moralism

'Merely moral' refers to art that promotes the concept of an ideal goodness that all mankind can recognize, acknowledge, and agree upon simply by looking deeply within ourselves or up to Jesus as an example. This concept may be true and biblical to some degree, since God's law is written upon every heart and echoes in every conscience.

But, what is not safe to tout as a Christian message is this: that this goodness which we may acknowledge by looking within or up to Jesus is actually achievable by us without 1.) God's saving grace; 2.) Jesus' leading lordship; and 3.) the presence and power of his indwelling Spirit. Without these, the Bible paints a much bleaker picture of mankind's ability and profitability when it comes to producing righteousness.

In fact, in the book of Isaiah, chapter 64:6 God compares humanity's best version of goodness to something like used tampons. Now, I know that for us, today, that may seem like an uncouth thing to say because of how insensitive it is to women. But, in the culture of the people to whom God first made this comparison, this idea was downright offensive; not to women during what was considered their time of "uncleanness," but to ceremonially clean, self-righteous men who were shocked to hear how spiritually "unclean" they really were.

The point being, in our depiction of mankind, modern

Christian artists must be careful not to overstate the potential of mankind's morality. The power is not "within us" and God's aim is not to get us to be our "better selves" or live up to our better nature. If we are going to label our art "Christian" or "Gospel" we must remain true to the Bible's portrayal of man as being fearfully and wonderfully made in God's image, but then, also, fully and woefully marred by sin; unable to produce anything good enough to gain salvation from God.

If this were not the case, God would not have had to produce sixty-six biblical books to help us get the point. The Bible would be fairly simple to write. In fact, it might have just read, "Try harder—The end."

However, it is because the Bible is such a lengthy work that there is sometimes confusion surrounding its message. Some of this confusion has created another side to this forth option of "Christian title, but no Christian function." This occurs when artists produce art that is branded as Gospel but that is actually Pre-Christian in theme. For case and point, I will be using the genre of Gospel music. Not because this principle shows up exclusively in that genre but, because in Gospel music, this principle is often (though not always) prevalent and easily demonstrable.

This discussion is not intended to bash any particular artist within the genre. It is, rather, intended to help artists see their way clear through some of the more difficult matters which must be faced when approaching the issue of faith and modern art. The following principles apply not just to music, but to stage and screen art as well.

The Gospel and the Old Covenant

When a Christian utilizes the arts, he can accomplish several things. He can share his unique perspective on life as a Christian with a particular background and outlook. Or, he can empathize or sympathize with the lost and dying world of which he was once an active part. He could aim to show the futility of a life without Christ. He might endeavor to draw attention to Christ's superiority over the best that this world has to offer. Or, if he is so inclined, he can do more than this. He can explicitly or implicitly convey the Gospel message. But just what is the Gospel?

It is interesting that you could ask five Christians this question and potentially get five different answers in return. However, if you were to ask the Bible that same question, you will get one answer; one long run-on sentence of an answer. Taken from a collection of biblical passages it might sound something like this:

God's Gospel is foolishness to those who are wise by the world's standards and it is seen as weak by those who are strong in themselves; it is not for those who are well but for those who are morally and spiritually too sick to help themselves; it is basically this, that Jesus Christ,

127

the son of God, unlike any other person who was ever born, intentionally came into the world and, he did this for one purpose: to be glorified along with God the Father by saving sinners (of whom I am the worse) from the wrath of God, justifying us by faith and graciously securing for us eternal and abundant life by making us sons of God and joint heirs with Christ who defeated Satan by his death on the cross and defeated death through the resurrection; and glory be to God, because no one will boast in their own power to save their self and none will be lost who are in the Father's hand; and, if any are lost, it is only because, like Judas Iscariot, they were never chosen, never called and never truly adopted sons but remained sons of perdition all along; they walked with those who walked with Jesus but, they themselves did not walk with him and were never truly known by him.

Now, the real question is, is the Bible's answer to the Gospel question the same or different than what most Christians would say? Even though no Christian would probably disagree with the run-on sentence you just read, it is odd that so many of us say such unbiblical things about the Gospel; things like, "Jesus died so that I could have a chance to be saved. Thanks to his death on the cross, if I live a saved life I will get to heaven. Glory be to God." But what this *really* means is that 'Jesus died so that I could have a chance to save myself. Glory be to me.'

Gospel means "good news." But, if I am responsible for getting my sinful self to "choose God" and then, after that, I am also responsible for "staying saved," this is not good news. My salvation is in jeopardy up until the moment I die. And as sinful as I am; as sinful as you are, if our salvation is in our own hand—we are doomed! But if, somehow, through all the trials of life, any of us do manage to "stay saved," then our salvation will be to our own credit, not God's. Many might deny that this is what they believe when it is put so plainly. But when they begin to explain salvation, they end up right back at this rendition of things.

How are so many Christians able to have such a 'works based' view of salvation? It is because much of what comes across as 'Gospel' is actually pre-Christian. In practice, many Christians have an Old Testament—if we will do this, then God will do that—theology. The Old Covenant was based on conditional promises of God and contained blessings which he would bestow, only if Israel walked obediently with God and lived by his law.

Some Christians today treat salvation like that old spiritual system. And this is not just in principle, for many still cling to the very promises of the Old Covenant. Quite a few churches teach this and some of our artists reproduce this teaching for us. This can be seen by looking at some of the most popular songs from the Gospel music world.

I was hit with this stark reality one day while listening to the local Gospel radio station. Two very popular Gospel songs came on, one right after the other. I imagine the DJ intentionally played these songs back to back because their themes were so similar. But, as I listened, their similarities troubled me.

The songs were Donald Lawrence's "The Blessing of Abraham" and Mary Mary's "Go Get It." The Lawrence song encouraged listeners to pursue the blessings that God promised Abraham when he first presented the Abrahamic (Old) Covenant mid-way through the book of Genesis. Mary Mary's song encouraged listeners to pursue individual blessing based on the "good life" that we are entitled to live by God's design of faith-plus-prayer mixed with performance-and-obedience—much like the Abrahamic Covenant.

These ideas are not alien to scripture. In fact, they represent important truths of the Bible. But it is just as important to understand in what sense these ideas are true and in what sense they are not. These artists were singing, as quite a few Gospel artists do, about the immediate, physical and material aspects of the Abrahamic Covenant. According to these two songs, the Abrahamic "inheritance" includes being lenders and not borrowers, starting businesses, writing books, scoring films, getting jobs and more. And all of this comes with the promise that whatever we touch is "anointed to grow."

But now we must actually open the Bible. And the second we do we notice that we have before us, not just the Abrahamic, or Old Covenant, but two covenants; or, rather, two testaments. A "testament" simply testifies to the fact that a covenant has been made. And there is a New Testament in our Bibles for a reason. But it is not the reason that many assume.

There is a new testament because a new covenant was made and we must ask ourselves, "What does this mean for the Old, or Abrahamic Covenant with all of its blessings?" And, "What does it really mean for Christians as heirs of the promise God made to Abraham?"

Some Christians function as if the purpose of the new covenant (or New Testament) was basically to help sinners successfully live by the old covenant and, thereby, obtain its physical, material blessings. Yet, this is not what the Scriptures say. Perhaps you are thinking of Ezekiel 36. There, God prophesied that, one day, he will make a new covenant with Israel and put in them a new heart; he will put his Spirit within his people and cause them to walk in his ways. And in that passage there is the promise of a physical land along with an abundance of food.

But we also know from Scripture that, by the time Israel becomes a part of it and finally gets with this new covenant, God will have already initiated and enacted it with the gentiles via the church (11:11-26). And, although we see God in the New Testament, lovingly supplying the needs of his children as any good father would, there is no mention of any grand-scale, immediate, physical or material entitlements for gentiles or the church as part of the new covenant.

This new covenant was, in fact, hidden within the old covenant and wrapped up in Abraham's seed—Christ. But the "newness" of it comes from its spiritual attributes over and above its physical applications. God has withheld the spiritual realities of the new covenant from Israel while, at the same time, withholding the physical realities of the new covenant from the church. And he will continue to do so until such time as he will unite all who are in Christ, Jews and Gentiles, together with all of the spiritual and physical attributes fit for the Kingdom of God. He has done this so that, between Israel and Christians, one group would not be perfected without the other (Hebrews 11:39, 40; Romans 11:25-32; Ephesians 2).

Furthermore, Hebrews tells us the difference between the Old Covenant and the New. In the Old Testament, we find, merely, the physical and temporal copies of everything that is revealed in the New Testament as "spiritual," "better" and "lasting." For instance, in the old, we find a physical people of God with a land prepared and blessed by God; along with a temple for worship and sacrifice; with prescribed sacrifices to be made. We find, also, a high-priest, a covenant and certain promises made by God which will be fulfilled by God *if* the covenant is kept by his people.

But, in the New Testament, the writer of Hebrews tells us that we have a better (heavenly) tabernacle, a better (heavenly) high-priest in the person of Jesus, a better sacrifice in the person of Jesus, a better (eternally lasting) covenant, and better (spiritual) promises which are not conditional. Paul also tells us in Romans chapter 9 and Galatians chapter 3 that, while the Nation of Israel represents the physical descendants of Abraham and pretty much failed to obtain or maintain the physical elements of the Old Covenant, we who are in Christ are Abraham's spiritual offspring and, therefore, immediate heirs of the spiritual portion of the Abrahamic covenant.

Once we come to understand the insufficiency of the physical elements of the Abrahamic Covenant; how impossible it was for the physical people of God under the best possible circumstances to produce the righteousness of the law in order to secure their blessing; how ineffective that old covenant was in producing anything other than Christ through Abraham's line, we will see how disturbingly sad it is when our presentations of the Gospel or Christianity today focus on the conditional blessings of that pre-Christian covenant.

God has not designed or ordained the physical elements of the Abrahamic Covenant to inspire

133

Christians to worship or move us to righteousness. He does not promise us those immediate, temporary, physical blessings as a reward for our faith. He has something far greater for all who are in Christ. And this "far greater" is Christ himself along with whatever he has prepared for those who love him. If eyes haven't seen and ears haven't heard what God has in store for us, how dare we produce any artwork, any song, script or sermon that depicts God's blessing as the mere material things of this world which are bound to waste away in this life (1 Corinthians 2:9; Matthew 6:19-21)

Deliverance vs. Salvation

Is it really good news? The idea that God is obligated to materially bless us if we live up to our end of the bargain; the thought that Jesus has fulfilled the law in our place so that we can have access to the physical blessings of the Abrahamic Covenant; is this a cause for song and celebration in the New Testament era? I do not believe that it is. But why is this pre-Christian Gospel so often preached today? It is because we often confuse two popular biblical concepts—deliverance and salvation.

When God originally proposed the Abrahamic Covenant and the Law of Moses, his people gladly received it as "good news" and responded, "We hear and will do" it (Deuteronomy 5:27). The blessings which lay on the other-side of their obedience made observing the Law and being faithful to God seem like a worthwhile task. But, over time, they saw how their sinful hearts transformed that old conditional covenant from good news, to bad news. Not that the covenant was bad, but it was bad for sinful human beings who could never be good enough to perform the righteousness God required (Romans 7:7).

But thankfully, God, in the Old Testament was a deliverer. He consistently delivered Israel from the many troubles they ended up in, largely, because of their own disobedience. When we read those accounts we gain comfort from seeing God's ability and willingness to save. He not only delivered them from temporary troubles; he also delivered to them very temporal blessings: e.g. manna from heaven; water from rocks; rescue from enemies; healing from serpents' bites, etc.

It is God's track record of delivering from these timely troubles and his reputation for delivering on these timely blessings that causes some Christians to view salvation today in very temporary, earthbound terms; as if it were merely deliverance. In their defense, it is easy to assume that salvation should mean the same thing to us as it did to the patriarchs of biblical history because, like us, they often used the words "save" and "deliverer."

But notice that, when the Old Testament uses the words "save" and "deliver," (Yashua in Hebrew = Jesus) it is almost always talking about physical, temporal rescue from some timely trouble. The exception to this rule is Messianic prophecies/passages. But when the New Testament uses the terms "saved," "deliver" and the name Jesus, it is almost always talking about mankind being saved from our spiritual and eternal problem of sin. Miracles are the exception to this rule. But even the miracles of the New Testament were not focused on deliverance but were, essentially, signs to point to Jesus's ability and authority to save from sin (Mark 2:9-12).

In the Old Testament, God did not place men's eternal salvation on the line with the Abrahamic Covenant or the Law of Moses aka the Ten Commandments. Those items were used to judge Israel's faithfulness and worthiness of the conditional promises of the covenant. And when they failed at this and ended up in harm's way, God moved to deliver them. However, salvation in the Old Testament was (as it always is with God) by justification through faith in the grace of substitutionary atonement—a sacrifice (Leviticus 17:11; Hebrews 9:22).

It is good to be mindful then that, in the Old Testament, God appears to be a deliverer. But he mainly used that entire period of history to set the stage for salvation, proving that something more than deliverance was needed. Deliverance only deals with man's temporary problems. If God is only a deliverer than salvation is left up in the air; up to our sinful selves and eternal security is out of the question. This is not good news because every person that God has ever delivered from any temporary trouble was/is still in desperate need of salvation.

Deliverance is good, but demons can return to those who have been delivered from them. God meeting my monetary needs this month is great! But next month I will have more bills. I could win the lottery but, according to Jesus, the rich will have many troubles in this life and will hardly enter the kingdom of heaven. I could triumph over all of my earthly enemies, but there is still the universal enemy known as Death, plus my own flesh and Satan himself staring me down.

On top of all of this, no matter what temporary victories we may have in this life, Christians are promised that those who wish to live Godly will suffer persecution. In fact, we are even called to suffer and God sometimes refuses to alleviate our pangs (2nd Corinthians 12:8,9). This is why Jesus told his disciples not to rejoice so much in deliverance; but more in the fact that their names had been written in the Lambs Book of Life—salvation (Luke 10:17-20).

Take a listen to your local Gospel station. Many "Gospel" songs sing of deliverance and glance over salvation. They bear the title but do not always perform the function. I am certain that there are socio-economic reasons and even historical, psychological reasons why African Americans gravitate towards messages of deliverance. Any oppressed people would. But, at the end of the day, salvation is the heart of the Gospel.

Because God is still a deliverer, it is through the Gospel that we will ultimately (even if not immediately in this life) experience deliverance from all that came with the fall of man. So, if an artist is going to depict deliverance biblically, it will be ***as a picture*** of salvation. This is what the entire Old Testament does as it points and looks forward to universal redemption (Isaiah 25:7). But deliverance and material blessing ***as*** God's gospel, his good news, is pre-Christian and should not be an option for Christian artists.

7. Grey Area vs. Black & White Issues

Why does it seem like white artists in other genres are free to drop their "Christian" title but when blacks do it, especially in urban music, there's always a problem? Isn't this a double standard?

In the previous chapters, I made a distinction between the Christian title and the Christian function as it pertains to art. I have also stated my opinion that we need Christians in every category from option number one all the way over to option number three. Still, it is my deep conviction as a Christian and as a sociologist, that there is a desperate need for certain people to do Christian art and to do it while bearing the Christian title. To be specific, I am referring to African American men.

It is socially significant and, therefore, even more unfortunate, when African American male artists shed and then fight against the Christian title. And yes, there is a different dynamic when blacks do this versus when it is done by whites. Since the dawn of the twentieth century, American art has had a philosophically rebellious, nonconformist aspect to it. Early on, this was not just in paint, but it grew in music as well. When white teens flocked to what was originally black music that became Rock & Roll, from the 1920's to the 1950's, it was often in rebellion to spite their parents.

The 70s and 80s was a time of extreme nonconformist art in music and film. During these years, the stereotype most often being broken by young, white, nonconformist artists was that of the 'suburban, middleclass, outwardly and overly Christian family with the pretense of piety and perfection' a la *The Simpson's* depiction of the Flanders' house-hold. The hippie movement completely shattered this happy myth. As Christian Rock took off, following after the broader culture, it became en vogue for white Christian artists to shed their Christian title. This is because shedding the title was one of the few nonconformist things these artists could do without actually sinning by fully assimilating into the culture.

The young, white artist, who was also a Christian, may have maintained his faith-fueled message and function, but by being willing to drop the Christian title, he could more convincingly prove himself to be a part of the generational nonconformist movement. Now, even though we are a long ways from the 70s and 80s chronologically, we are nonetheless still very influenced by the cultural shifts of those days.

Many of those philosophical currents still hold sway today and can be used to explain the current dynamics between young white Christians and modern art. For decades now, there has been a desire and effort among young whites to break the tamed Ned Flanders stereotype and to communicate the message that the Christian title is not as important as the Christian function.

A Black Thing

But, there is not the same problem with young African American males. Neither the Christian title nor the Christian function is socially, stereotypically associated with them. Typically, older African American women are presumed to be church-going, hat-wearing, tithe-giving Christians. But the usual preconception of young, black men is either one of illegal activity, ignorance or else Islam as the hope.

So, then, when black men do away with the Christian title, rather than coming across as nonconformist and stereotype-breaking art; it, instead, reinforces the stereotype that young black men have a problem with the church or with Christianity or with Jesus or the whole ball of wax. Therefore, when we see this clipping of the title, as in the case of young blacks from within the Christian Hip Hop community, it raises a different set of antenna than when young, white, Christian artists make the same separation of faith and art.

On the other hand, when young, black, Christian males who are strong in their faith proudly affix the Christian title to their art, especially Hip Hop art, it is indeed counter-cultural. It is a statement in and of itself that says to others, "Contrary to popular opinion, it *is* possible to have a vibrant life in Christ as a young African American male." And there are very many people who still need to receive this message.

Continental Drift

Is it possible that Hip Hop's relocation to the South has caused a change in the culture's stereotypical religious identity? And if so, has this change now caused young black Christians to have some of the same concerns that young, white, Christian artists have been reacting to? Consider this, in the North where Hip Hop began, the popular religion of choice for urban African American men has, since the late 60s, been anything but Christianity. But in the South, where Hip Hop now has its headquarters, Bible-belt Christianity has held on as the religious way of life.

So, while the idea of young black men engaging in Christian Hip Hop in the North has always been counter-cultural, it might not be so in the South. And, it just so happens that the popular Christian rap artists who have relinquished the Christian title are they who hail from the South. Perhaps, these Southern artists see the need to prove that they (and their art) are not simply Christian in name like much of the traditional southern culture, but Christian in deed; in function. Wouldn't this justify these young, black men dropping the Christian title from their art?

If nothing less, this would be a much better explanation than what has been put forth so far by the formerly known as Christian rap regime. However, even this can and should be tested for truth. For, currently, even in the South's Bible-belt, the stereotype concerning young, black men is not that they are only outwardly Christian while they inwardly have more tradition than truth. That characterization might be aimed at the Bible-belt as a whole, but not at the South's young black men.

If there is any stereotype that needs to be broken concerning African American males and Christianity in the south, it is that they will only find themselves at the altar of the Christian church once they have spent their strength and given their best years to sin and Satan. Or, that they are only in the church to financially fleece the flock or sexually seduce the sisters.

So then, even when we look at the need to address the Bible-belt's stereotypes concerning black males, it seems that the solution would not be to abandon the Christian title for the sake of art but, rather, to wear it young; wear it proud; and wear it well. That is, after all, what brought the Christian Hip Hop community to the place that served as the Launchpad for its biggest names to date.

Matters of the Heart

The challenge of wearing the Christian title well is, perhaps, what will scare many away from choosing this route. Option number two (Function but no title) or number three (no title and no function) are much easier to live with. In those categories, where the artist operates without the Christian title, no one has any expectations and, so, any spirituality or Christian content that happens to seep through is like an added bonus.

And, if the artist's lifestyle is not in full accord with Christian ethics, there is no harm and no foul because the artist is not claiming to be doing "Christian art." In fact, he may not even have exposed the fact that he is a Christian at all. On the other hand, if an artist claims Christianity for himself and also for his art, there is immediately a high standard against which the artist's efforts can be measured: his morality, modesty, purity, sincerity, charity, family, and artistry will all be under someone's microscope.

Under these circumstances, it is understandable why some artists might want to relieve themselves of the Christian title. This way, they will not be judged too harshly when they fall and prove what should have never been forgotten in the first place—that they are human and, therefore, sinful.

However, because scripture warns us that the heart is deceitful above all else, artists must also be mindful that the strategy of letting go of the Christian title could easily stem from a desire to get away from accountability in order to wallow in what artists should never forget—that they are human and, therefore, sinful.

Black Christian Men: A Work of Art

I have defined art as the attempt to answer the cultural question, "What's worth reproducing?" If this is accurate, then art that is designed for a certain demographic answers the question, "What's worth reproducing in a certain culture or society?" This should help us to understand why artists in the inner-city, producing art for the inner-city, might have a different responsibility than do artists producing art in Hollywood.

When films are produced, with their array of characters, voices, perspectives, plots, subplots, texts, subtexts and themes; they are produced for a wide range of audiences. Any number of people can watch the same film and each find something in a different character that they find worth reproducing in their own lives. Great movies have the ability to transcend culture and time; they show us what is worth reproducing everywhere and throughout all time.

Because of the wide range of potential for that medium, in my opinion, it is difficult to put such stringent demands on African American, Christian actors making Hollywood films. Though, in the next chapter, I will address certain precautions which might apply. But, generally speaking, we do put a lot of demand on the roles played by black men.

We all remember the Blaxploitation films of the 1970s. In contrast, almost every African American smiled the first time they saw a movie with an African American president (before the dawn of Barack Obama). We understood that, though these films were telling the broader American culture "What's worth reproducing," there was a special message contained in the media for young blacks watching those images.

Hip Hop, and even Christian Hip Hop, has a similar responsibility. Though every rapper or urban artist may desire to produce an enduring work of art that transcends his own time and culture, he will, nonetheless, be speaking most directly to that young African American who looks to the artist to answer the cultural question of art the most; because the artist looks just like him. Even though whites might listen to rap music just as much as blacks, young whites mainly look to Hip Hop art to answer the aesthetic cultural questions (fashion, music, lingo); yet young blacks look to Hip Hop art to answer the ethical cultural questions of values and ultimate meaning.

As an African American, Christian male who helped to create the counter-culture of Christian Hip Hop and who still works with urban youth and young adults, I definitely see the need for urban artists, and in particular black men who speak to Hip Hopper culture, to demonstrate their appreciation for and connectivity to Jesus Christ and his people by bearing the Christian name. Because the artist who is able to skillfully and successfully do this, is himself, a work of art and something worth reproducing.

8. INDECENT EXPOSURE: CURSING, SEX SCENES AND THE ART OF EUPHEMISM

If it makes the point more convincingly, or makes the art a more believable imitation of life, how far can Christian artists or, artists, who are Christians, go in order to convey their message?

This honest question was put to me by a rap artist in Florida who had recently recorded a song which, in his opinion, needed explicative language in order to be most effective. However, this question is not just being asked by rappers. Actors and scriptwriters are also concerned with issues such as this. Though, we must acknowledge that rappers and actors do not have quite the same struggle.

While it is understood that actors are often limited in their creative control and locked into the scripts being handed to them; and scriptwriters have to take into account the narrative, metanarrative, under and overtones of their message; rappers are usually much more free and direct in choosing and delivering their own lines.

Film is an interesting medium. With film there is visual and not just audio input; there are different camera angles; there are numerous actors and scenes; and a rewind button which allows us to go back and study all of these features. There is, therefore, always a chance to go back and catch something that we missed before. There is an art to being able to write a script (or a song) in such a way that the viewer catches enough to be satisfied the first time around, but can find new or deeper meaning on the second, third or any number of subsequent views as well. Often times, subtlety is the key to this.

Since, this is the way film works, Christian actors and scriptwriters must tap into a great deal of ingenuity in order to bring their faith to bear on their art. But, as we said in chapter three, ingenuity must be met with just as much intentionality. For actors, this means looking for roles that present such an opportunity. And these opportunities hardly ever come without some kind of compromise. Take, for instance, the blockbuster film *The Book of Eli*. Many Christians heralded the movie as a proponent of Christian faith. But in the end, the artistic message was that, not only the Christian faith, but faith in general was worth reproducing.

The ethical trade-offs associated with this roundabout way of bringing together one's faith and art have presented Christian artists with the questions now before us. Specifically, how does the Christian artist depict or deal with songs or scenes that communicate spiritually or morally problematic answers to the cultural question of art? More specifically, how does one deal with songs or scenes of unjustifiable violence, profanity or sex.

I will focus more on profanity and sex scenes since they raise problematic issues. I say this, not because I believe that senseless violence is less harmful but, rather, because violence can be acted out whereas profanity and sex must be, to some extent, actually performed in order to be captured, as far as film is concerned.

Profanity

Should the Christian artist curse? Before we consider this, we must clear up what we actually mean when we refer to someone "cursing." After this we can evaluate the Christian's use of cursing in day-to-day life. And then we can decide where the Christian ought to stand on the issue of cursing in the arts. In answering these questions, there are three categories of 'cursing' to keep in mind: Condemnation, Offensive Language and Course Joking.

Condemnation

In the first category, we say that someone is "cursing" because in the truest, most potent sense, that is exactly what the person is doing. When we curse something, we condemn it. To say, "God damn (<u>anything</u>)," is literally to call upon God to condemn someone or something. Think about that for a moment. Is this something a Christian can justifiably do? The disciples of Jesus once wanted to call down fire from heaven in judgment against Samaritans who would not receive Jesus on his journey to Jerusalem. But Jesus rebuked them (Luke 9:51-56).

It is not our place to judge anyone or anything to the degree of condemnation. In fact, we are told, in all things, to give thanks. Not *for* all things, but in all things. If someone cuts me off in traffic, I might momentarily want to condemn that person. But who am I? Are there not a million more horrible things for which I myself should be damned? If God is gracious to me, how then am I not able to give grace to someone else in this instance?

The challenge to not condemn people, and even things, helps us to learn humility. I am not God. I do not know how God may work this horrible thing which has happened to me out for my good or the good of someone else (2nd Corinthians 1:4). So, for me to condemn something without knowing the totality or finality of

God's will is, in effect, me playing God. It is the height of pride and profanity. This does not mean that there are not damnable things in this world. Jesus condemned anyone who would hinder a child from coming to him. But it is he who condemns, not we.

Offensive Language

The second category to consider when dealing with the subject of cursing is Offensive Language. Even if we imagine a scenario where a Christian could use strong or explicative language to curse something or someone without profanely "playing God", the Christian must still consider who his audience is and who he might offend. Paul advised that all things are lawful but all things are not expedient or beneficial.

So, even if my conscience truly does not bother me and I am able to use "colorful" language around a certain group of people (like African-Americans who use the debated N word around other African-Americans); still, if I know that my speech will be heard in mixed company and there will be some in that company whose conscience will not allow them to hear my strong language without being offended, then (as a Christian) I must put away all such communication for the sake of not offending my brother (1st Corinthians 8).

Corse Joking

The third category of cursing is Course Joking. This includes the traditional four letter words as well as crude or lewd jokes. Even if someone argues that it is possible to use curse words without actually meaning to condemn anyone or anything; that would not change what the Scripture says, "Every empty or idle word will be judged (Matthew 12:36)."

This biblical truth might, in fact, put the one who is cursing in a different kind of jeopardy. If we use condemning language but do not actually mean to condemn, we are wasting our words. And not just wasting them, but wasting them on communicating crass ideas which we are commanded against (Colossians 3:8). When the scriptures inform us that fresh water and salt water do not come from the same spring; it is to encourage us to be wells of useful, living water and not dual faucets for lukewarm communications. Therefore, the Christian has no business wasting words by cursing or coarse joking in day-to-day life.

Cursing in First Person Perspective

With this understanding in mind, we can now consider whether or not the Christian can/should include cursing in his/her artistic productions. First, we will consider the Christian artist (or the artist who is also a Christian) who is speaking from the first person point of view.

Speaking from the first person perspective, the Christian only has the ability to condemn that which God has already condemned. And such condemnations ought to come across as "God's judgment" and not the Christians. We know that God has already condemned sin. And we know that all men and women are sinners and worthy of condemnation. In fact John 3:18 tells us that "Whoever does not believe in the Son of God is condemned already." However, we cannot know with certainty, from this side of eternity, which individual sinners will be saved and which will be forever condemned.

And so, the range of things that Christians can condemn, artistically or otherwise, is pretty slim. For example, a song line which sings "Today started off great/ but then I missed work cuz the damned was late." Or "Damn it! I can't sleep/ neighbors at it again/ heart aching, glass breaking why won't she leave that man?" This condemnation is not a Christian sentiment because it is God's place to judge, not ours.

But suppose the Christian artist is not actually judging but, simply expressing how she feels about a certain experience; and she truly feels like condemning the source of her struggle. If this is how she feels, should she censor herself? Won't her art seem unrealistic if she tames her tongue? I think a better question to ask is this: won't her Christianity seem unrealistic if she does not tame her tongue (James 3)? Self-control is the fruit of the Spirit. The inability to exhibit this fruitful display says just as much, if not more, about her soul than would her explicative laced artistic expression.

She must remember that those who live in Christ no longer live unto themselves but unto him who died for them and rose to live again. Therefore, we regard no one, not even ourselves after the flesh. As much as the Christian's experience may be the same as the non-believer's, it ought to also be very different in some key ways.

This does not stop us from feeling like condemning our bad experiences or those who have caused us to have such experiences. But it informs our total estimation of those experiences. We are not here to simply emote and show the world that we know what it feels like when life sucks.

We are here to illustrate that though we may be able to empathize; still "we are afflicted in every way, but not crushed; perplexed, but not driven to despair; persecuted, but not forsaken; struck down, but not destroyed; always carrying in the body the death of Jesus, so that the life of Jesus may also be manifested in our bodies (2nd Corinthians 4:7-10). So, even as artists, when speaking from the first person perspective, it is not our unsanctified souls, but the life of Christ in us that is worth capturing and reproducing.

Scriptwriting/Story-telling and Acting

If, however, the Christian is acting out the role of someone who would most likely use condemning speech, then he is not actually condemning anything or anyone; and so, he is not guilty of "cursing" according to the first category mentioned above.

But since the artistic question is, "What events and experiences are worth reproducing?" We must ask, 'Is the man who condemns his troubled life, or his enemies, or aspects of his past, or his estranged family members, worth reproducing?' When we watch these types of artistic portrayals, do we sit in the cinema and cheer "Yes!" when the twenty-something year old male who grew up without his father finally gets to tell his dad "F#@k you!" to his face? (Some in the audience may actually cheer at this.) Even though the Christian artist playing this role is not actually condemning anyone, he is still illustrating an idea which might translate to his audience as, worth reproducing.

This is especially true if there is nothing else within the artistic presentation to challenge this depiction. This will be the message that impressionable audiences are left with. But at this point, someone will argue, "That's how life really is. The scene would not be realistic without this kind of unbridled and unchallenged confrontation."

But it is helpful to keep in mind the old saying about the cyclical nature of life and art. 'At first, art will imitate life. But then, life will imitate art.' When watching the screen, audiences are looking into a mirror. Sometimes they wish to see their reflection; but at other times, they leave to go reflect what they have just watched. Therefore, the Christian must be careful about what he helps his audience to view as 'worth reproducing.'

Having said this, I do believe that it is possible for a Christian to act and perform in such a condemnation filled, confrontational scene, if the overall point of the movie is to the contrary of his character's profanity. The theme might be the need to learn grace or forgiveness, reconciliation or some other admirable idea. This could overturn the negative narrative. When dealing with the medium of film, we must keep in mind, not only the text, but the subtext; not simply the narrative, but the metanarrative (the story behind the story).

The film could be out to depict the idea that the character that is vulgar or violent will have to reap what he sows as he comes to a violent, vulgar end. In this case, the theme might be humility or divine and providential justice. Therefore, before evaluating the contribution of the Christian who employs curse words in an artistic portrayal, we must first consider the overall artistic point or the production.

If a Christian does take such a role, he might try to ensure that the prideful or profane character he plays is not painted in a completely positive light; or that the character is morally corrected by other characters or providence sometime before the credits roll. But he will likely have a hard time accomplishing this.

Gone are the days of the morality plays of old or the virtue-versus-vice based plays of Greek theater, which gave us our modern cinema. Today, in our society, there is no clear divide between good and evil. We have come to terms with the fact that no one is thoroughly virtuous and, also, that no one is fully evil. And so, in the modern media, our good guys are a little bad and our bad guys are a little good.

It is, therefore, unlikely that the role of the baddish-good guy will receive too much moral correction before the credits roll. This makes the Christian artist's job harder in choosing roles; especially if he is going to be concerned about the messages he sends in his art. But it will help him to remember that the art of acting is not just telling a good story; it is telling a good story about what's worth reproducing.

Offensiveness in Acting and Story-telling

Even if it is possible for the Christian artist to portray a vulgar or profane character without actually conveying the idea that the character's vulgarity and profanity is worth reproducing, the artist must still concern himself with the second category of cursing – offending his hearers. This one is not easy to get around since the artist cannot control who will hear him using this colorful language all for the sake of art.

This is a dilemma for many Christian writers and actors. An artist might be trying to convey the idea that a woman's negative circumstances have led to an unexpected positive result. But how to portray her negative circumstance and a realistic depiction of the woman's reaction to it without having her use condemning language; this is the challenge. And so, the profanity will likely proceed despite whoever might be offended.

As far as movies go, ratings systems might help with the "Offensiveness" issue. If a viewer knows that his or her conscience will be offended by the use of explicative language, the rating system will serve as a warning that a particular movie might need to remain off limits to him or her.

But, what does this do for those viewers who desire to see good art; who appreciate the telling of a good story, good cinematography, acting and directing; but who, at the same time, wish to not be offended by profanity or vulgarity? Must these viewers miss out on good movies simply because of their moral sensibilities?

On top of that concern, what about the Christian artist whose conscience is not helped by the arguments above. To him, cursing on camera is no different than cursing in the day-to-day life. His conscious is bothered because he feels that he is, at the very least, being asked to disobey the scriptures that warn against filthy communication and coarse joking. According to the Bible, it would actually be sinful if this individual were to employ cursing in his art; not because of the cursing itself, but because he has violated his own conscience (Romans 14:23).

How could we help these individuals? I believe there is a way. But I doubt that many will have the courage to do something as drastic as this. One way to address these issues would be with the use of audio or theatrical censoring. In this approach, the explicative language could be partially written into the script; but either before the words are fully spoken, or in post-production, the words would be cut off by the lines of another actor in the scene or cut out (bleeped out) by editing software.

What this does is, in effect, sanitize the script. So, for the sake of staying true to reality, the words or ideas are present. But, for the sake of the meta-narrative (the story behind the story), even while the artists are acknowledging and portraying that this colorful language is common, they are also conveying that it is not worth reproducing.

This would also save artists from being guilty of the third category of cursing – Course Joking. By sanitizing the script this way, artist would not have to actually say the words because there is no actual intention to have anyone ever hear the words. The same could be said for musical compositions.

Formerly-known-as Christian rapper Sho Baraka demonstrated this in 2013 on his soul searching and thought provoking album *Talented Xth*. The project is a perfect example of a Christian toggling back and forth between option two (Christian function but no Christian title) and the border between the middle-ground of common grace and option number three (no Christian title and no Christian function).

The album was marketed as both a Christian project and a general market album. It did contain a few songs which would definitely register as Christian art. Yet these songs sat amidst others which could have been a Christian's art or, just as easily, the art of a non-Christian. As a Christian's art, it was refreshing to hear a Christian think/speak on the issues addressed in the album, even if not necessarily from an eternal perspective.

Twice on the album, the artist tangles with the "B" word; you know the one women used to hate to be called. Both times, as he comes up on the word, Sho does a bit of self-censoring. In the song, "Michael" he talks about a woman who is "a self-proclaimed Bad __." But he censors himself in two ways. By prefacing the "B" word with the phrase "self-proclaimed," Sho has taken the 'curse' word out of first person speech and put it in the moth of another character. Also, before he actually gets a chance to utter the offensive word, another character interrupts his verse with an admonition to, "Watch yo mouth homie." By these measures he is double protected.

In another song, *Jim Crow*, the artist does not stop himself from saying actual word. However, he does leave the first person perspective and put the language in the mouth of a social opponent. Elsewhere in the album, another artist comes close to cursing in first person but censors herself as well.

However, we must be careful here. It begins to border on licensciousness if these tactics are toyed around with in the name of fun or freedom. It is poor leadership for artists who are also Christians, speaking in first-person, to lead their listener's minds up to the point of cursing and then stop short. The artist believes he is "safe" because he has not cursed, yet he has led his listener to the edge of a cliff and slammed on the breaks. He may stop himself, but his listener is already falling.

Sex Scenes – Free Cheating?

We can apply some of the same principles above to this next discussion. But there are some specific concerns when dealing with the issue of sex. Whereas violence can be acted out and cursing can be edited out, sexual scenes must, to some degree, be actually performed if they are to be believably portrayed. But before we can talk about on-screen intimacy, we must talk about off-screen intimacy or sex in general.

Sexual intercourse does not just begin at the point of penetration. What is generally considered "foreplay" is actually sexual arousal. With the rapid beating of the heart, the body's involuntary directing of the flow of blood, the secretion of bodily fluids and the stimulation of body parts, the body has begun to prepare itself for the act of sex.

There are several ways we may look at this issue biblically. We might simply ask the question, should the Christian artist be in the practice of preparing him/herself for the act of sex with an individual that he or she is not married to? The Bible is clear that it is best for a man not to touch a woman who is not his wife (1 Corinthians 7:1 NKJ). There is no need to go stirring up passions, such as the sex drive, which will be terribly hard to bring back under control.

The rebuttal will come, "But it's not like every person who does a love/sex scene ends up actually having sex with that person." To which I would respond, 'this is true. But it has happen frequently enough.' Ask any number of Hollywood sex-scene couples how their off camera romance was fueled by what the movie director demanded of them when the cameras were rolling. After being married to actress Demi Moore for only a short while, actor Ashton Kutcher referred to performing in love/sex-scenes as "Free cheating."

Can God keep a Christian artist from falling into this sexual snare? Yes; of course he can. Should the Christian go about putting him/herself in these types of situations banking on God's ability to come to the rescue? No; of course we should not test God in this way (Luke 4:12).

On top of this, remember that through art, we are ultimately answering the question, "What's worth reproducing?" Most of the time, sex scenes are not between married couples and so, this aspect of the relationship being portrayed is not worth being reproduced. But even with a married couple, because sex in marriage is sacred, it is beyond worth reproducing. It is worth being kept private. We need not contribute to our society's voyeurism, as if viewers have no idea of what married couples might do in private.

Dirty Dancing?

The issue of sex in art, or sexually arousing art does not just pertain to actors and actresses. Dancers too must wrestle with this question. There are many styles of dance around the world which, in some way, artistically reproduce the primal instinct of sex. Some of these dances are integral to a particular people's way of life. But can Christian dancers reflect the ways of these cultures as they pursue their craft?

I think this question is best addressed if we remember to ask the other cultural questions along with the issue of cultural art. If a culture is answering the question of art, (What's worth reproducing?) and at the same time answering the question values, (What do we do to perpetuate our way of life?), and develops a style of dance that pays homage to the act of sex while encouraging and celebrating their mating rituals, then they have connected their art to their values. In fact, for some cultures, dances that we would call "provocative" are reserved for weddings celebrations in order to serve as instruction and inspiration for newly married couples.

It is common for other cultures to mimic these dances. Sometimes this is done to pay homage to one's heritage. But it is just as common, especially for us in America, to take such cultural artifacts as these dances, and to take them out of context in order to spice up our own artistic portrayals. It is no secret that, where we live, sex sells. So, rather than using such dances to celebrate our culture's perpetuation and the proper place for procreation, we use them to indiscriminately arouse passions and praise pleasure no matter the context or consequences. We too have linked the questions of 'art' and 'values' only, we do not have strong answers to the 'values' questions. And it shows.

There are many ways in which sex is displayed as 'worth reproducing' in modern dance which should cause concern for the Christian artist. One particular instance of this is in Hip Hop dance, i.e. break-dancing. Often in b-boy battles, dancers will use the simulation of sexual acts to embarrass their opponents. Many Christians have expressed regret after getting caught up in this cultural practice in order to win competitions or the respect of clapping crowds.

But, as Christians, we should be quick to connect our values to the question of art whenever we are taught or tempted to perform sexually explicit dance moves. Because of our values, we not only know *what* is worth reproducing; we also know *when* things are worth reproducing and when they are not. There may be a time for Christians to display that they can skillfully move their bodies in provocative ways, but that time is most likely, only when they are with the one person whom they are free to sexually satisfy and not simply tempt and tease and then leave unfulfilled. And, in case there is any doubt, I am talking about in marriage.

The Art of Euphemism

But sex is a healthy part of life and a major issue in any society. How does the Christian artist capture this fact without violating wisdom or conscience? One helpful strategy to employ when dealing with this topic would be to remember the concern of the Apostle Paul. He desired that believers should be as ignorant or innocent as little children when it comes to actual evil, but not ignorant or naïve when it comes to Satan's schemes (1 Corinthians 14:20; 2 Corinthians 2:11).

Our goal, then, if possible, when it comes to "adult activity" or things which could cause others to stumble or sin, should be to acknowledge without advertising. This way, we can speak to those who are 'in the know' without unnecessarily informing those who do not need to know.

To accomplish this, artists must become acquainted with and skilled in the art of euphemism—saying it without saying it. Some years ago, I wrote a song entitled "Pyramid Schemes." The second verse of the song dealt with online pornography and masturbation. Several lines from that verse could serve to illustrate the point. Speaking of the pixilated pornographic images, I wrote:

In a trance you watch those tiny dancing dots/ you know whatever this is romance is not/ it's just an imitation/ your only participation is hand-to-eye coordination

So, instead of talking about watching and masturbating, the term "hand-to-eye coordination" creatively makes the same point without having to actually spell it out. This is not simply a tool for songwriters. Scriptwriters have creatively employed this tactic as well. In the Will Ferrell film *Anchor Man*, instead of a sex scene, the male and female co-stars are shown riding a pair of animated unicorns through a fantastical, colorful landscape called "Pleasure Town."

Similarly, in the blockbuster film, *Sucker Punch*, each time the star (a young girl) is forced to dance provocatively and strip-tease for her clients, or else be abused by her keepers, we are not allowed to see her sexually arousing dance moves. Instead we are taken inside of her mind where she battles numerous opponents with deadly martial arts skill; the metaphor—through dancing she is fighting for her survival.

We do not have to be lewd or crude or curse to convey a strong message. And, when we feel that these things "must needs be" as Jesus once said concerning horrible sins in the world (which he followed with "But woe unto them through whom these things come) there may be a way to euphemize any indecent activity without euthanizing our audiences or our testimony.

But, if something must die, let it be the dying of ourselves to our rights to advance our careers by "any means necessary." Our Lord warned that whoever signs up to follow him must be willing to take up their cross. And, he also promised that if we lose our life, or lands, or families, or careers or anything else for his sake, we will actually not lose but, gain it and much more (Mark 10:29).

9. Unequally Yoked

Can Christians partner with non-Christians to produce Christian works of art?

This question came up after speaking to a group of high-school students in upstate New York. As things wrapped up, the event MC asked the Dj, a Christian pastor, to put on some exit-music. The first song the Dj played happened to be the intro from the *Church Clothes* mixtape by Lecrae. The MC, who was a Christian youth leader, remarked several times throughout the course of the night that he loved Lecrae's music. As the teens exited the building, the enthusiastic youth leader began to chime in (on the microphone) with what was coming across the speakers. However, he was not quoting Lecrae. Instead he shouted repeatedly, "The Cannon!"

"Cannon" refers to the Hip Hop Dj and producer, Don Cannon, the self-proclaimed number one co-signer of what's hot in Hip Hop. The *Church Clothes* mixtape, which he hosted and endorsed to the Hip Hop world, was peppered with Don Cannon's incessant signature self-endorsement (the repetition of his own name).

Now, the youth leader echoing "Cannon" at this event had no idea that he was co-signing the number one co-signer of what's hot in Hip Hop. But almost every New York teen in the room did. They hear "The Cannon" endorsing Lil Wayne, Two Chainz and many other godless influences in their lives. The looks on their faces said it all. Even though the event was over, there was now a world of confusion that someone would have to address if these youth were going to be successful at living out the messages they had been receiving all weekend about surrendering everything, even their music playlists, over to the Lord.

But, perhaps, hearing from "The Cannon" at this event was a good thing. Maybe some of those youth, who were getting ready to leave the event, still skeptical about Jesus, were further convinced to consider him after hearing an endorsement from Don Cannon, someone they have been culturally conditioned to trust. Isn't this a positive thing? I would say "Yes," if there was not also the danger of violating a very clear biblical principle of not being unequally yoked with unbelievers. But we will see that the danger is not necessarily where we often assume it is in these types of sacred-secular connections. But there is a danger, nonetheless.

The Christian and AT&T

Many Christian artists throw a fit whenever 2nd Corinthians 6:14 is brought up in this context. The contention usually goes something like this, "If I work for AT&T, they're not a 'Christian' company; so does that mean I'm unequally yoked at work?" This they say supposing that the individual who has brought up the passage will only be satisfied if Christians only ever speak to, acknowledge and deal with other Christians. But not only would it be nonsensical for one Christian to want such a thing of another, it would also be unbiblical and, practically, impossible.

In John 17, Jesus prayed for his disciples and all those who would eventually believe in him through their witness (us). In doing so, he specifically asked the Father not to take believers out of the world. In 2nd Corinthians 5, Paul says that if we were trying to avoid dealing with sinful people altogether, we would have to leave the world! His point being that this is an impractical idea. However, Jesus did pray that we would be in the world but not of it and that the Father would sanctify us in it. Through this sanctification, men would know that we belong to him.

So the question becomes, how do we remain in the world, dealing with unbelievers because we will simply have to (whether we want to or not) and yet remain sanctified? One of the answers to this comes from the

Corinthians passage, "Do not be unevenly yoked." But what does this mean?

The language of being yoked comes from agrarian culture. Farmers, especially in the time period of the writing of Scripture, depended on animals to plow fields. Strong burden-bearing-beasts such as oxen were linked to one another by wooden neck-braces which forced them to move together. Once yoked, the animals would walk side-by-side dragging a plow through a field, doing the farmers work for him. There is something about this picture that God through Paul is commanding believers to avoid. What is it?

Perhaps it is doing our heavenly Father's spiritual work together with unbelievers? i.e., plowing his fields in order to plant seeds in the souls of men. Or, maybe, it is connecting with unbelievers in a way where we are unevenly matched, i.e. where the non-believer has more say in the relationship than the believer. Or, more severely, perhaps, the warning is against being linked to unbelievers in any way at all. If this is the case, Paul is saying that whenever we become linked with unbelievers in anyway at all, the relationship is automatically unequal because of their ability to corrode and corrupt the believer's affection and devotion to God. Let's look at each of these.

Is the Problem, Being Yoked in Anyway At All?

No, not 'at all,' for Paul continues to make his point in 2nd Corinthians by asking, "What fellowship does light have with darkness? Or the Temple with idols?" Obviously this is a rhetorical question and its answer is, "None." But it is not strictly, 'none' because he also communicates that we would have to leave earth in order to literally accomplish such a feat. Also, we see in the Gospels that Jesus ate with "sinners." When asked why he acquainted with them, Jesus responded, "It is not the healthy who need a physician but the sick." This serves to instruct us that there is, at least, one biblical motivation for believers to do more than simply 'tolerate' unbelievers but to be present and engaging in social interaction with them, as Jesus did. But this reason is medicinal and for the unbeliever's good, not for the Christian's advancement. Besides, in social settings, the believer is not yoked. A yoke implies the inability to leave the context.

But there are any number of circumstances where a believer might feel that he is actually yoked. Suppose the Christian basketball-player on an NBA team takes a survey and finds that only four of his team-mates are Christians. He is, in a sense, yoked with his team. But, again, he is not yoked in the true sense of the word. For the bond between them is not inseparable. If ever he begins to sense that he would be forced to disobey God because of his association with the ball-club, he can remove whatever tie that binds them, even if he is penalized by the league for doing so.

Now, there is a sense in the Bible in which God's people are expressly forbidden from being yoked with those who are not God's people. This is especially the case when God forbids Israel from intermarrying their children with the children of neighboring nations. (Deuteronomy 7:3,4; 1 Kings 11,2) In these cases, in such tight knit, intimate affairs, God seems to be saying that there is no way that "yoked" will not lead to "unevenly yoked," so do not do it! The danger here was that these binding relationships would lead to the hearts of Israelites being turned away from God to idols. Concerning the arts, this may have implications for Christians in dance troupes, musical groups and close partnerships.

Personally, after being in a music group with no less than four members for fourteen years, I can attest to the fact that being in a group is a lot like being married to several people at once. And I can only imagine the compromise and temptation one would face while being the Christian minority in such a group. The Christian in this circumstance must have a good sense of his own personal mission as one of Christ's called and chosen people. If he has this, he could possibly influence the mission of his musical group so that the cooperate function does not take him away from his personal, spiritual goals. But if he is going to be serious about his faith without contradicting it, he must think long and hard about the realistic likelihood of being able to accomplish this while being so tightly tied to unbelievers.

Is the Problem, Being Unevenly Yoked?

Having said this, believers should be careful not to enter into contractual arrangements which make the penalty for breeching any clause so severe that the Christian is left feeling he can never decline to perform what is being asked of him by the unbeliever(s) with whom he has entered into a legally binding agreement. In such a case, the believer would be yoked in a spiritually unhealthy relationship due to three things: the seemingly inseparable nature of it; the imbalance of power; and the incompatible interests of the two parties. This takes the relationship from yoked to unequally yoked.

In the 2nd Corinthians 6:14, Paul is drawing from an earlier passage of scripture in Deuteronomy 22:10. The imagery is of a farmer putting a yoke around two significantly different animals. Not simply different in size, but in species. In the case of a size difference, the smaller one would be forced to do whatever the larger one does. If the larger one wants to rest, the smaller must rest. If it wants to work, the smaller must work, for it does not have the strength to go its own way whenever the two directionally disagree.

But based on the Deuteronomy passage, it is not so much the difference in size as it is the different in species. The two beasts being yoked together will have two very different sets of instincts and interests; and therefore require different means of motivating them to move. This will complicate any plans the farmer has to use them at the same time and for the same purpose. And so, because of their different natures and desires (one having a new nature and the other, still the old), the Christian and the un-believer will be unevenly matched in their appetites, attitudes and actions in several important aspects. Therefore, the list of what the believer and the un-believer can participate in together is not endless.

Does this limitation call for a separation in every situation? Suppose I work for a non-Christian boss at AT&T. It's the end of the year and I find myself engaged in an inner-office debate on whether or not we should rename our annual Christmas celebration. Some people want to call it a 'Holiday party' instead, since they do not really celebrate Christmas. We cannot decide and so we take a vote which results in a tie. That is, until my non-Christian boss begins to wield his weight and swings it in favor of renaming the celebration a 'Holiday party.' He is my boss, and he has more power than I do. In this situation am I unevenly yoked? Is the Apostle Paul telling me to quit my job? Maybe not.

But, suppose I am a musical recording artist and I have just signed a contract. I now owe my new record label three albums over the next two years. Time goes by and the first album does pretty well but the label is convinced that it could have done a lot better. They want me to be less vocal about my faith or, perhaps, team-up with a mainstream artist who does not share my values. I am adamant that I do not want this other artist on my next project which I have poured my heart and soul into. Yet the label is determined to feature her.

After getting nowhere in our discussion, the label exec. pulls the trump card and reminds me that, under the terms of my contract, he has the final decision. Because they have financed and own all of the material I have produced over the last year, they are going to do what they believe will bring them the best return on their investment and so, they will feature the mainstream artist on my album whether I like it or not. And they will release the song whether I complete the project or not.

In the first case, working at AT&T, I was simply, personally disappointed by my boss' decision. But I was not forced to do anything that was truly ungodly since, forcing people to verbally acknowledge Christmas is not a work that God has called us to perform. In the second case with the contract, not only was I "yoked" and bonded to unbelievers but I did not have the power to go my own way when the spiritual distance and difference between our competing interests surfaced. The issue of purity and maintaining a good name and testimony — these are things that we are called to.

The Problem is, Being Unevenly Yoked on Spiritual Matters

This leads me to believe that it is not just being yoked or even unequally yoked (though that can have its problems too) but rather, the problem is being unevenly bonded together with unbelievers to accomplish things that God has only called believers to do.

When the believer goes to work in God's field, to plow his ground and plant salvation's seed in the hollowed out hearts of men, it will be very important that this work is not done in a way that will corrupt the seed planting process. Jesus talked about the complications which are already facing the Gospel seed: people trampling on it; rocky ground; and thorns choking out whatever little bit of growth that does happen to occur. These represent the cares of life, desires for riches, hard hearts and Satanic, stealth missions to steal away the seed from the soil.

With all of this already at work against the Gospel, why would we complicate the mission by bringing in ill-natured animals to help us to plow the field? This does not mean that we cannot work with unbelievers. And it does not mean that we cannot utilize their services. As a rapper, and as a member of a two-time Grammy nominated rap group, I have made good use of gifted musicians, studio engineers, CD manufacturers, distributors and retailers who were not Christians. But how do I justify engaging in such partnerships, without violating the principles we have just discussed?

Simple. The idea of being unequally yoked does not forbid the use of someone's service who is not a believer. Rather, it forbids us from being linked together in any way that allows the characteristics or nature of the one beast to conflict or compete with the nature of the other which has been called by God to plow his field and bear a different type of burden. Anytime these contrasting characteristics come up and confuse the message of the Gospel or its implications, the believer is unevenly yoked.

This is where things begin to get a little tricky for modern artist in search of a standard. But the standard should be to, at least, restrict partnerships with unbelievers to a level where whatever help they may give, be it musical composition, song arrangement, artistic direction, wardrobe, etc. does not offer an occasion for the expression of the unbeliever's contrary wisdom, nature and desires.

Having said this, I do believe that we ought to look for every opportunity to partner with other believers. Have you ever noticed that Paul's command in 6:14 is not simply, "Don't become unequally yoked?" Rather, it comes right in the middle of two passionate pleas (one right before it and one right after it) for the Corinthians to open up, extend and enlarge their hearts toward other believers. It is not just about who believers shouldn't get yoked to, but rather who they ought to yoke with; i.e. other believers—especially believers who, as in Paul's case, were getting maligned and mistreated because of their commitment to the Gospel mission. This is who we ought to be doing business with!

The Glory and the Platform

There are two more important cautions when considering this issue of Christians becoming unequally yoked with non-Christians for the sake of art. To be yoked is to have two animals share and bear the same burden. But there are two things which believers and nonbelievers cannot share: the glory and the platform.

The Glory

First, the glory cannot be shared. It would be one thing for two humans, a Christian and a non-Christian to divide the glory for a successful art project between themselves. But this is not the Christian's goal. While the unbeliever is out to get glory for himself, the believer is out to capture glory, all of the glory for God. But what does this look like, both biblically and practically?

Biblically, we can look at the account of the father of faith, the chief patriarch of the nation of Israel, Abraham. In Genesis 14, Abraham went to war, along with his friends who, presumably, did not worship the Most High God as did he. This war ended up helping the king of Sodom. However, Abraham only went on the expedition to rescue his relative Lot who lived in the king's territory. Once victorious, Abraham was visited by the king of Sodom and Melchizedek, priest of the Most High God. After he alone was blessed and he alone gave an offering to the priest, the king of Sodom said to Abraham, "Give me the people you recovered and you can keep all of the goods and riches for yourself."

But Abraham had a philosophy that, I think, will help us in our current discussion. He told the king, "No. I will not take anything from your hand. Not even a shoestring. I do not want you to be able to say, 'I have made Abraham rich.'" Think about that for a moment. Abraham did not get involved in the war for riches. For him, it was a rescue mission. And, on top of that, Abraham knew that God had far more in store for him. Because he knew that God was up to something greater, he did not want the glory/credit to go to someone else who was disconnected from his God, when his story was eventually told.

To see this issue of 'shared glory' practically, we can look at a hotly debated topic amongst urban Christian artists — the issue of musical production. Namely, should

Christian artists seek/select musical soundscapes for Christian songs from non-Christian producers? The Cross Movement, the group of which I was a part for most of my musical career, had set a standard in the Christian Hip Hop world that has been misunderstood by many who have followed after us.

When we expressed our own stance and cautioned others against seeking production from non-Christians, it was never an across the boards, "You should never do it!" In fact, most of us (if not all) believed that there was a way to do it without becoming unequally yoked or jeopardizing the mission. Far from thinking that Christians should not use music produced by non-Christians, we believed strongly that the Christian should be mindful of the 'glory issue' and careful not to take musical production from producers who are well-known, especially if they were well-known for wickedness or providing a platform for wickedness.

The thinking was that, if a producer is world renown, and if his fame is antithetical to the believer's overall message, not only will it seem a contradiction to have the producer's name associated with the Christian's work, but it would only further reinforce a stereotype that needs to be shattered; namely, that the Christian and/or the Christian God is too weak to rise from obscurity on his own and needs the help of someone who is a bit stronger, more established, and able to properly prop the Christian up on the celebrity stage. We firmly believed that, this was not the kind of representation that God desired; especially from someone who has made a career of dishonoring God.

A popular Christian artist once responded to this reasoning with, "But in the Bible, God often used secular rulers to bless his people. Look at King Cyrus who blessed Ezra and company with permission and provisions to go back and rebuild the Temple and the walls of Jerusalem." While this is true, we must also recognize that anytime God used secular rulers this way, it was in the process of humbling Israel who had repeatedly done evil in the eyes of the Lord. God moved Cyrus to take pity on Ezra and his people. But before God's Nation was a disobedient one, God often told the leaders of Israel that he wanted to be the only one ruling and providing for them. He was quite clear that he did not want his name to be profaned and that he would not give his glory to anyone else. (Isaiah 48:11,12)

This does tie into the theme of not becoming unequally yoked with unbelievers. Like Abraham, we must keep in mind the story that is being told. What was most important in his eyes was not just that God was up to something, but the way in which the story of how God accomplished that 'something' would be told. Rather than have an ungodly king become known as the reason for his success, Abraham desired not to be unequally yoked with him in the pages of history. May we be mindful of this concern as well.

The Platform

Aside from the issue of shared glory, there is the issue of the shared platform. In chapter six, I touched on the way Christian artists will endeavor to find common-ground

184

with unbelievers, searching to find areas of life that are common to both in order to create dialog through artistic conversational pieces. There is no conflict of interests in that approach. The interests are actually, genuinely shared even if the ultimate viewpoints between believers and believers are divergent.

The problem arises when the Christian artist (even the artist who is also a Christian) invites the unbeliever onto a shared platform in order to speak on spiritual matters, matters about which, the non-Christian and the Christian cannot agree. In this case, it is just as dangerous for the Christian to vouch for the unbeliever as it is for the unbeliever to validate the Christian. To understand why, once again, let's take a biblical look at this issue; followed by a practical one.

In Psalm 50:6, 7, God, through the psalmist, challenges the wicked person with, "What right do you have to recite my laws or take my covenant on your lips? You hate my instruction and cast my words behind you." The entire Old Testament is set to several melodies and meant to be sung. Therefore, God could have just as well said, "What right do you have to sing my songs?" He threatened to tear such unworthy individuals apart via divine judgment!

In this psalm, God was speaking to the wicked among those who were his people by name. How much more are the unsaved not qualified to sing his songs? In Philippians chapter 1, Paul wrote that, even if someone preaches the Gospel with ill intentions, at least Christ is preached. And so, we say, "Amen" whenever Christ is being accurately preached, no matter by whom?

But we do not "amen" when the preaching of Christ is confused or contaminated by the unholy source of the preaching. This same Paul became annoyed with, and cast a demon out of a girl who was telling the truth about the Gospel and its presenters. In Acts 16, the demon in the possessed girl kept calling out, "These men are servants of the Most High who are telling you the way to be saved!" But the whole town knew that this woman was possessed. Rather than have a demoniac continue to vouch for their ministry, Paul had had enough and would have no more. To continue to allow this demon to speak truth through the girl would only strengthen people's trust of and reliance upon the demon-possessed girl on other spiritual issues. And this was unacceptable.

Practically, I could share a memorable experience from my days as a Christian rapper. In 2002, conscious rapper, KRS One began working on his attempt at a Christian rap album entitled *Spiritually Minded*. Be it the growing Christian rap market, genuine respect for the genre or his own professional felt-needs, for one reason or another, "The Teacher," as he has dubbed himself, believed it was time for him to step into the Christian rap world.

Before this point, KRS had spent years doing what he could to discredit the Bible and Jesus Christ, both on and off the mic. But, perhaps, this project would be different. In the process of putting it together, KRS contacted my group,

The Cross Movement and asked if we would like to collaborate with him on a song.

While we were excited to hear from him, we declined the offer for four main reasons. One, we knew that the album would likely amount to a metaphysical mixed bag of religious world-views (which it did indeed turn out to be) and we did not want to contribute to anyone's spiritual confusion. Two, we did not want to mislead KRS or anyone else into thinking that we (KRS and us) were all "spiritually minded" in the same way.

Three, we did not want to lend whatever credibility we had to sanction KRS as a trust-worthy source on spiritual matters. Not only on the project in question, but into the foreseeable future. As Christians in the arts, we must consider, to what degree we are responsible for the messages put forth by the messengers we co-sign. And although we cannot predict what another artist will do in the future, at lease with certain artists, (specifically other Christians) we have some degree of sound reason to believe that we will not end up regretting our collaboration.

Lastly, we knew that KRS One would have the ultimate say in what messages were conveyed on the album. We would not have veto power but he would, and considering our very different nature's, spiritually speaking, that would have been the epitome of being unevenly yoked.

Generally speaking, Christians and non-Christians can, and often do, partner together on the areas of life which fall under common grace. And, I believe that, if we are able to partner on these common grace areas in life, we ought to be able to do so in art, as well. But it must be maintained that, while both Christians and non-Christians can have hope and faith, we do not have the same hope since we do not have the same faith (because hope springs from faith). So, faith is not a common grace area shared by believers and unbelievers; not artistically, not metaphysically, not realistically or hypothetically. Therefore, any yoke in this department will automatically be uneven and, if uneven, biblically barred.

10. Quality Assurance: Excellence and Christian Art

As Christians, shouldn't the art that we produce be of higher quality than that of a world full of unbelievers?

There is a sense in which the answer to this question is indeed, 'Yes!' But, in another, more sobering sense, we are forced to respond, 'No; not necessarily.' Right away, I know that there are some who will disagree with me. The thinking is usually something like this: We are God's people; commissioned by God to do his work; we have God's Spirit within us, 'preparing our hands for war' as it were. Doesn't this guarantee our position at the pinnacle of the artistic panoply? But again, my reply is, not necessarily.

Remember that the cultural question of art is twofold. It is first essential and then esthetic. Essentially, the question is 'what subjects are worthy of reproduction.' Esthetically, the question is 'how expertly or uniquely can this be done.' I believe that, because of the Christian's access to and confidence in biblical truth, we ought to have higher or better answers to art's essential question. But because of God's purposes in the direction of human history, I believe that art, esthetically, may be raised just as high by non-Christians as by Christians.

There are three factors which play into my position on this issue. First, we must consider what God does for both believers and nonbelievers alike, which ensures a certain level of quality in almost everyone's art. Second, there are things that both believers and nonbelievers can do on their own to enhance the quality of their art. And third, there are things that God does to raise specific individuals to prominence in order to forward his purpose and plan in the earth. And, in these cases, an individual's art can become the beneficiary of this divine activity. But this, too, can occur with believers and nonbelievers alike. Let's look at each of these more closely.

What God Does for People in General

Does God only give gifts and talents to those who are believers in Jesus? If we are talking about Spiritual gifts, then the answer is "Yes." But when it comes to gifts and talents in the natural realm, these are indiscriminately dispensed and dispersed to the children of men, believers and non-believers, throughout the world.

When God created mankind, he blessed them and told them to be fruitful and multiply. God was not simply blessing their ability to have children. God blessed them to be productive in general. This "blessing" was to guarantee a certain level of success as men and women used their natural God given abilities to respond to the cultural mandate. These abilities (and the blessing upon them) did not vanish when sin entered the world. Like the natural treasures and resources still buried deep within the unredeemed earth, the ability to excel in numerous natural talents is still buried deep within unredeemed man.

Scripture informs us that God is pleased to give rain and sunlight to the just and the unjust. Rain and sunlight are needed in order for crops to grow and these good things are indiscriminately supplied to all by the benevolence of God. This is the "common grace" which was discussed in chapter four. From this we learn that God does not withhold life's necessities from humanity until individuals come to Christ. But, neither does he withhold life's niceties from us until we seek salvation. Hence, the ability to skillfully perform tasks or produce great works of art is one of those universal niceties we enjoy by God's common grace.

Have you ever had the privilege of witnessing greatness, a skill or talent developed to the highest level? Take, for example, Michael Jordan playing basketball in his prime; or any other top performer executing a particular skill at the height of their career. If you have, it is doubtful that you critiqued the performance or production by saying, "He would be so much better at this if he was a Christian."

You might have said that it would be better, meaning more spiritually beneficial, if the production were serving a higher purpose by being properly directed to the God who gave the artist the skill in the first place. But that is a much different statement which might be true essentially. However, esthetically, there is no denying that it is God who has given and blessed the skill; even if the artist is not giving the skill back to God.

The Faustian Bargain

Someone might ask, "But can't Satan also give people natural talents if the person makes a 'deal with the Devil'?" Biblically, the answer is 'No'. Satan can empower people with supernatural abilities; such as the performing of miracles (doing what is not natural; e.g. fortune telling, and the like).

Satan is also just as likely to nullify natural abilities, (e.g. demon possessed individuals are often out of their minds and behaving madly). Biblically, what Satan gives is either supernatural or sub-natural and dehumanizing. But when it comes to natural talents, he gives nothing.

What Satan *can* give, in the natural realm however, is

success and position. Paul called him the god of this world. As the god of this world, Satan took Jesus up to a high place and showed him the all the kingdoms of the earth. There, Satan told the Lord, "All of this is mine and I can give it to anyone I want to; I will give it to you if you will bow to me." Satan had something to give, indeed. But he was not able to offer Jesus any talent or ability.

Satan wanted Jesus to use his own abilities, but to surrender them to Satan's service. However, Jesus knew that by wielding his own abilities correctly, he would end up legitimately possessing all that Satan wanted him to obtain illegitimately.

Think about that. An illegitimate path to success based on natural abilities used wrongly is what Satan wanted for Jesus. That is also what he desires for us as he tempts us to misuse our talents and abilities for his gloomy glory. But Jesus did not bow and we do not have to either. Everything that comes from God, including all talent and ability, ought to be returned to him as it accomplishes the purpose for which he gave it (Isaiah 55:10,11; Deuteronomy 8:17,18).

It is, therefore, a slap in the face of God when we see artists who are at the top of their game, skill wise, and then, credit their excellence in art to Satan. Even if the artist is well versed in wickedness, one does not have to make a "deal with the Devil" just to excel in art *and* exceed in sin.

But, even if we were to accept the Faustian Bargain and surrender our skills to Satan in order that he might reward us with his crooked kingdoms and lowly lordship, nonetheless, the natural talents being negotiated in that bargain would still be God-given, even if Satan-driven.

What People can do for Themselves

Another reason why I do not believe that the believer's art is guaranteed to be of higher quality, esthetically, than the un-believer's art is because of what each artist can do on their own. When it comes to spiritual gifts, believers are told to fan into flame what has been deposited in them. The same thing applies to natural talents and learned skills. Whatever our beginning stages, as believers or unbelievers, we can increase in our ability to execute and master our various crafts.

Natural talents are those heightened abilities that we are born with. To be able to carry a tune, draw images by hand, move our bodies in wonderful ways to musical compositions or compose such compositions for others, etc.; these are natural gifts given to us that we in turn give back to God and/or God's world. These talents can be honed and enhanced until they reach expert levels. Learned skills are other abilities that we pick up and through much training and practice, we can become the best in a particular field of applied science or art.

Every true artisan, every skilled craftsman who has ever produced an enduring work of art will likely testify that success did not come easy. Behind every minute of production and every inch of canvas, there were hours, days, maybe weeks and possibly even years of sweat and tears poured in.

And even before their masterpiece was produced, there was training and trying then trial and error; creating and self-critiquing then exhibition met by crushing criticisms from others. They will tell you of the personal sacrifice and self-doubting but also of the belief which they held onto when almost no one else believed in them. Through all of this, we see the artist's dedication and determination.

To the degree that each artist invests in his or her craft, we will see the development of their particular skill or talent. If a Christian invests much less time and energy into her natural talents than another artist who is not a believer, will the fact that the one is a Christian make up for her lack of preparation and dedication? Christians may give one another a pass for producing half-hearted, cheesy, subpar, unoriginal and unimaginative works of art; but any objective observer will rightly judge the lackluster presentation for what it is.

The Motivating Factor

But, what if the Christian and the non-Christian put just as much time into developing their talent; won't the Christian come out ahead in that case? Once again, this is not necessarily so. However, there are two reasons why we might be tempted to think that this would be the case. The first being, we believe that the Christian ought to have a higher motivation for his art and, based on that higher motivation he ought to produce a better product; one worthy and reflective of such a high motivation.

Consider what the driving or motivating factors for his art might be. The Christian has been confronted with divine truth; has objective (biblical) moral standards; a relationship with the God of the universe; can draw from all of biblical history; has the Gospels and the epistles to shape his worldview; and possesses the indwelling Spirit of the God of creation. How, then, with all of this can the Christian fail to be less creative than his nonbelieving counter-part?

This is a compelling argument. But consider what possible tributaries might flow into the unbeliever's motivation for developing his talent. His art might be his way out of poverty; it may be the only way to express the anguish in his soul concerning some past experience; or, searching for a sense of significance, his hope might be that his art will catapult him out of obscurity and into notoriety; out of a love for money and power, he may pour himself into his art in order to, one day, enjoy the lifestyles of the rich and famous; driven by ego and pride, the artist may truly feel that he is the best in his field and will not rest until he is proven to be so; beyond any of this, the non-Christian artist is still a person, made in the image of God and has a natural inclination to creatively express the supernatural design after which his soul was fashioned.

These are also powerful driving forces. Now, on the one hand it can be argued that, just as much as motivating the artist, some of these factors could stifle or corrupt the artist's creativity. But, on the other hand, it can also be argued that the Christian artist could be motivated by some of these same factors. So, unless or until we are able to know each artist's true motivation, and the positive vs. negative impact of each motivating factor upon the artist, it will be impossible to know if any of the afore mentioned factors have hindered or helped the caliber of the artwork.

So, even if we assume that the Christian is only motivated by the purest factors, and the unbeliever motivated by the most base; still, depending on the level of their natural giftedness, honed ability and the impact of their motivating factors, an unbeliever could do his best and submit a final product that is higher in quality than the best efforts of a believer, as far as the aesthetics of the piece is concerned. The spiritual condition of the two artists is no guarantee that one of them will have an esthetically better "best" than the other.

Old Testament Ethic

The second reason why we often think that the Christian's art should be better than the non-Christian's is because, as I mentioned in chapter 6, unfortunately, many of us have an Old Testament understanding of "success," "blessing," the Kingdom, and the purpose and plan of God.

In the Old Testament, success was visible, material, physical, earthly, temporal and often, judged by the same standards as the neighboring nations nearby the people of God. But that version of "success" did not produce the righteousness and faith-filled lives that God required or desired.

In the New Testament, however, the success that is secured for us is, most of the time, intangible, non-materialistic, promised but postponed and often pre-empted by pain. It is not earthly but heavenly, though, also, it is lasting and eternal. So, then, rather than being seen through their outer condition and superiority, the success of God's people in the New Testament is seen in their inner contentment and spirituality (1st Timothy 6:6).

However, since God is the same yesterday, today and forever, we should be able to look in the Old Testament and see some of this ethic as well. And, indeed, we can. Biblical Israel was not without poets and artists. When we read the Pentateuch (first five books of the Bible), we are reading what was originally an artistic work. The Psalms and Proverbs, too, contain musical and poetic devices. But were the Hebrew's law-codes, psalms and proverbs artistically any better than their neighbors'?

Actually, they were not. They were largely in the same format and some scholars believe that Israel made a habit of copying the layout, design and, in some cases, even the wording of certain stanzas from their Near-eastern neighbors. What set Israel's art apart was not the esthetic aspect of it, but rather, it's essential nature. It is the fact that the content of Israel's art was directed to or by the LORD that set it apart.

But why doesn't God just allow his people to flex skillful superiority over the unbelieving world? The New Testament tells us why. God is often pleased to put his immensely valuable treasure in "jars of clay" so that it may be clearly seen that the true value lies in the treasure, not the jar (2 Corinthians 4:7). God will not allow us, with all of our creativity and uniqueness, to eclipse the grandeur of his great gift. God desires to confound the wisdom of the world and put to shame the pride of the world; to demonstrate the weakness of the world's strength and to nullify the affirmations of the world (1 Corinthians 1:20-31).

Because of this, what is seen as foolish often becomes a choice tool in the hand of God. This is not to suggest that the Christian artist should plan on producing weak and foolish presentations of faith-based art. It is only to caution us not to put a whole lot of stock in anything that God has already determined not to base the success of his mission on.

Does God deserve our best? Absolutely! Esthetically, it only makes sense for us to give him our all and for our art to illustrate that we have done so. When we do not give our best, our all, it communicates that God is not worthy of it.

This is key because, our unbelieving counter-parts (who have been gifted by the same God as we) are giving their all for that which is no god at all. So, if there is any justifiable competition or comparison between the believer and the unbeliever's art, it is not in the outcome, but in the input. Because of our worthy Subject, our dedication and commitment to excellence should rival and surpass the unbeliever's dedication and commitment.

But we must always be mindful that God is out to communicate and demonstrate the fact that *he* gave *his* all. And that fact is what he is counting on to win men over, not our excellent art that blows the competition away.

What God does for Specific Believers and Specific Non-believers

If God has indiscriminately dispensed various natural gifts and talents to both those who will become believers and those who will not; and the level of skill that these talents may reach is, fundamentally, not a spiritual matter but a practical one; then how do we explain passages in scripture and instances in life where God, or someone else in the spirit realm, seems to be responsible for supernaturally enabling and ensuring the success of an individual?

It does not take in-depth cultural analysis to discern that there are some people who seem to be unusually elevated in their sphere of expertise. There are also people who may not even be exceptionally talented but who, nonetheless, end up exceptionally elevated. Sometimes these people are Christians; many times, they are not. It is tempting to rush right to a spiritualized explanation as to why this might be. But there are other potential contributing factors to consider before we examine the possible spiritual causes behind this elevation.

One thing to keep in mind is that success, in today's media-based brand of modern art, is largely just a mixture of timing, technological savvies and a willingness to debase, efface or otherwise expend oneself for the amusement of others. In 2012, Korean artist Psy took the internet world, and then the international world, by storm with his online video "Gangnum Style" which racked up over a billion views in just a few short months, though most viewers had no idea what the artist was saying.

Beyond simply catching the bored online world at just the right moment, there are also those who are gifted in the techniques of marketing and promotion. Either by pushing or paying their way, they can secure a spot on the public platform for themselves or for the artists they represent.

But, aside from the one hit wonders or short-lived careers of those who only succeed for a season, there are others who come onto the scene and hold their spots for what seems like forever. I, like everyone else in the world, was stunned on the day that Michael Jackson died. Not simply because we had lost him. But, because I had forgotten that we *could* lose him. His larger than life legacy had all but persuaded me that he would never die and that his long career could never come to an end.

Some people, like Jackson, have clearly earned their spot at the top and, for the most part, we do not question their reign. Others, however, hold their title while we are hardly able to hold our tongues as we wonder, 'why him?' or 'why her?' And when we can come to no reasonable conclusion, we wonder if, perhaps, there is something more; something spiritual at work behind the scenes.

Biblically speaking, I have already addressed where it is that talent comes from and where it does not come from. Satan does not have talents to give. The popular theory that he was a master of music or worship leader in heaven is not a biblical truth. The passages in Isaiah 14 and Ezekiel 28 which mention "Lucifer," "cymbals" and "pipes" refer to the pomp and satanic pride of an earthly king, not an angelic musician. Furthermore, Genesis 4:21 tells us that a man named Jubal was responsible for giving the children of men stringed and piped instrumentation, not a fallen angel. But, even though Satan does not have talent to give, he still has position and power to give away.

But not only Satan; we know from Scripture that God also raises individuals, whether talented or not, into prominent positions for such a season as this or that, in order to fulfill his plans and purposes. We have both positive and negative examples in the scriptures where natural talents and attributes are augmented by divine activity in order to accomplish God's will.

On the Plus Side

Positively, we think of Esther who, because of her natural beauty, was selected to become a part of a foreign King's haram from which he would choose his new queen. On top of her natural beauty, she underwent twelve months of the kingdom's beauty enhancement and preparation. She received advice on how to best be pleasing in the eyes of the king. And this was not "Christian" or "Biblical" advice; but very practical training in whatever talents seemed best in the eyes of those who were responsible for preparing her.

However, before she was even selected to become a part of the king's haram, it was the godly guidance of her cousin Mordecai which aimed her in that direction. Once there, the Bible tells us that she won favor in the eyes of the king, and everyone else, so much, so that she was eventually crowned queen. Later, Mordecai tells her (and us) that this was not of her own doing or for her own good. Rather, she was selected to learn the talents needed and was then placed in that high position, primarily, for such a time that she could best serve God's purpose in delivering his people.

Consider also Daniel, of whom the bible says, "An excellent spirit was in him." Because of this excellence, he was preferred by the Babylonian king and put in charge of over 100 other servants. It is tempting to think of this "excellent spirit" as something alien; something foreign to Daniel's own personality and attitude of the mind; as if, a spirit-being that specialized in excellence somehow entered Daniel and caused him to perform his tasks with superb distinction. But this is not the case. It is Daniel's own spirit that is referred to and characterized as "excellent."

When Daniel and his kinsmen were captured and carried away, they were selected from among the children of the ruling and noble classes. They were selected, first of all, because they had no physical defect, were good looking and already had a high aptitude for every kind of learning (Daniel 1: 3,4). These were natural attributes and talents which Daniel and his friends had cultivated, even before God's favor came to rest on them.

God's favor does, indeed, kick in; but only after their commitment to God is made clear. After standing out because of their natural giftedness, they begin to stand out because of their spiritual commitments. We begin to get the sense that God may have had something to do with the stunning results of their religious dietary experiment. But not long after, we are told for sure that God began to add extra ability on top of their already natural giftedness.

Though Daniel and his friends already had a high aptitude for all kinds of learning, God gave them knowledge and understanding of all kinds of things (Daniel 1:17). And to Daniel, he gave the ability to understand visions and all kinds of dreams. As a result, the king found none equal to them among all of his magicians and enchanters. They were, in the king's eyes, ten times better; ten times more talented than everyone else.

But Daniel shows us what is really going on. In chapter 2, the king has a dream, the details of which, he will tell no one. Yet he demands that his dream be interpreted. No one can guess what it was and because they cannot guess it, they cannot even pretend to interpret it for him.

The king was prepared to put his magicians, enchanters, sorcerers and astrologers to death because they could not help him. But Daniel and his friends prayed to God. Then Daniel was given the king's dream and its meaning. He went and told the king. But he also reported something that, even we today, can learn from as we discuss the issue of faith, art and excellence. To the king Daniel said, "This dream and interpretation was not given to me because I have greater wisdom than any other man alive."

In other words, it was not Daniel's talent or natural giftings that God, somehow, suddenly accelerated due to the fact that Daniel was a believer. No. God did something supernatural in Daniel because **1)** he wanted the king to know what the dream meant and, **2)** God wanted the king to know that there is a God in heaven who does what no man, not even Daniel by his own wisdom or talent, could ever do (Daniel 2:27-30).

From this we learn that God uses our natural talents and abilities, but only to an extent. However, when he is after supernatural results, he does not rely on our natural abilities; not even if they appear to be ten times better than everyone else' in the eyes of others.

Addition by Subtraction

How about negatively? Does God ever grant talent, ability, power, position or supernatural success to those who do not and will belong to him, in order to accomplish his purposes? To this, we would have to say, "Yes." When Daniel miraculously received the vision and interpretation of the king's dream, he praised God saying, "Wisdom and power are yours . . . you depose kings and raise up others . . . . (Daniel 2:19-23)."

And this is exactly what we see. In the book of Daniel, King Nebuchadnezzar of Babylon is raised up by God to punish his people Israel. Yet in Isaiah 45 we see that God will also raise up and use King Cyrus of Persia to free his

206

people from, and punish, Babylon. In fact, we are told that God would strengthen and stay Cyrus' hand.

Also, we see Pharaoh persecuting the people of God in the book of Exodus. But we learn more clearly in Romans chapter 9 that Pharaoh was raised up by God, only so that God could show his arm strong against the hard-hearted ruler. In fact, Paul tells us that God has the right to make out of the same lump of clay, a vessel for honor and a vessel for dishonor. From this we learn that there is not much difference at all in the people God uses, be it talent-wise, power-wise or other-wise. The real difference is the purpose for which God uses them.

So, then, no one's talent is any more necessary to God than anyone else'. Neither is anyone's talent more fit to be blessed by God or used by God than anyone else'. God, as the potter, can take from a lump of clay and make a beautiful vase and, from the same lump, take and make a beautiful ashtray. It is God's handiwork either way and when considering what he has done, each vessel will be quite beautiful in its own light.

What separates them is their function. One is to hold flowers; the other, to hold ash. The ashtray might be designed to hold a significant amount of ash and might, therefore, be larger or taller; it might even be more beautifully crafted than the vase and attract more attention because of its esthetic state. But what is essentially inside the two vessels says all that needs to be said. There is no way that the charred ash of human accomplishment in the ashtray will be more valuable or more beautiful than the flower of the Gospel inside the vase.

Art – A House for Beauty

David said there was one thing he desired: to dwell in the house of the LORD and gaze upon the LORD's beauty (Psalm 27:4). Though it paled in comparison to the God's beauty, the house of the LORD was beautiful itself. In Exodus 31, God told Moses that he had sent his Spirit to give Bezalel all knowledge and ability to artistically design the Tent of Meetings which would contain the Most Holy Place, the place where God would meet with his people. God then told Moses that he had given to all able men ability that they might make all of the vessels and ornaments needed for proper worship.

But the book of Hebrews tells us that all of those things, in all their beauty, were just copies of the true reality which surrounds the LORD in heaven (even though it is he who surrounds all things - Psalm 139:7-12). Right now, God is making his people into a new, true work of art, a building that will house his beauty forever. In the meantime, he continues to give ability to all able men and women in order that we might artistically make those things which are most suitable to honor his presence. Whether or not people actually use their gifts for God's glory is a different matter. In the end, we will see that it is God who uses us for his divine purposes regardless.

So then, when we see artists atop the platform, with stardom and success, conducting the current flow of human history, we must not be so quick to credit Satan with the nonbeliever's success and God with only the believer's. Neither should we lose heart when it seems like the Christian artist's talent never nets him what is so easily secured by the unbeliever's unsanctified abilities.

The true difference between them is not based on the level their talents may reach or the secular success they might achieve. It is, rather, the purpose they serve in God's plan and the value and beauty of what is placed in their vessels and offered to the world.

Complete Christian Art Options Chart

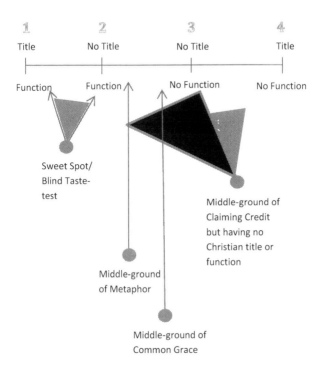

1	2	3	4
Title	No Title	No Title	Title

Function   Function   No Function   No Function

Sweet Spot/
Blind Taste-
test

Middle-ground of
Claiming Credit
but having no
Christian title or
function

Middle-ground
of Metaphor

Middle-ground of
Common Grace

Made in the USA
Charleston, SC
07 March 2013